When Autumn Comes

When Autumn Comes

✦

Creating Compassionate Care for the Dying

Mary Jo Bennett

iUniverse, Inc.
New York Lincoln Shanghai

When Autumn Comes
Creating Compassionate Care for the Dying

iUniverse books may be ordered through booksellers or by contacting:

iUniverse
2021 Pine Lake Road, Suite 100
Lincoln, NE 68512
www.iuniverse.com
1-800-Authors (1-800-288-4677)

Cover Design: James Bennett
Author Photograph: Anne Danahy

ISBN-13: 978-0-595-31662-5 (pbk)
ISBN-13: 978-0-595-76470-9 (ebk)
ISBN-10: 0-595-31662-X (pbk)
ISBN-10: 0-595-76470-3 (ebk)

Printed in the United States of America

"We abhor and reject the moment when we will confront the nearness of our death. But the dying stage of our life can be experienced as the most profound growth event of our total life's experience. The shock, the pain and anxiety are great, but if we are fortunate enough to have time to live and experience our own process, our arrival at a plateau of creative acceptance will be worth it."

Death: The Final Stage of Growth, Elisabeth Kubler-Ross, MD

To Roger who saw me through the tears;
To Fiona and Oliver—the fruits of my heart.
And to James—whose companionship, while living and dying, quickened my soul.

Contents

A NOTE FROM THE AUTHOR

While all of the incidents in this book are true, the names and personal characteristics of the individuals involved (with the exception of friends and family, where permission has been given to use their names) have been changed in order to protect their privacy. Any resulting resemblance to other persons, living or dead, is entirely coincidental and unintentional.

PREFACE

When Autumn Comes: Creating Compassionate Care for the Dying is an insightful and tender book that will be of value to anyone who spends time with the dying or someone with a serious illness. It provides a realistic introduction to caring for the dying as seen through the eyes of a hospice volunteer.

Every death is different. *When Autumn Comes* shares realistic stories of fifteen people who die from a variety of conditions. The stories are carefully chosen to illustrate themes that a caregiver or volunteer may encounter. Family dynamics, pain management, disturbing symptoms, and unexpected humor are all recounted with compassion and a matter-of-fact realism that can only be gained by bedside experience. In addition to recounting episodes as a hospice volunteer, Bennett shares vignettes about her own experiences with the death of loved ones to help us understand how our own experiences influence attitudes about dying.

Each chapter includes helpful trigger questions to encourage readers to think through issues that may affect their own caregiving. This feature of the book makes it a handy learning tool for volunteer training programs as well. Other useful reference materials include a list of terms used in hospice work, a bibliography of selected readings, and a list of online resources to learn more about hospice care.

Caregivers and hospice volunteers provide essential human contact and services that are a fundamental part of caring for the dying. Although compassionate human contact requires no special training or medical degrees, it is often in short supply within medical systems. Health care reimbursement plans generally do not think of companionship or practical support as medical services. As a result, in many cases those who have the most contact with a dying person are volunteers or unpaid caregivers.

The National Hospice and Palliative Care Organization (NHPCO) estimates that in the United States 500,000 people volunteer in the nation's 3,200 hospice organizations annually, providing more than ten million hours of service each year.[1] Looking beyond hospice volunteerism, a recent national random survey in the United States found that more than one-fourth of adults said that they had provided care for a chronically ill, disabled, or aged family member or friend in the past year. That would work out to more than 50 million volunteer caregivers, many of whom provide care with little or no support from anyone else.[2] This book is an invaluable aid for those who find themselves facing this challenge.

Hospice volunteers serve in many different ways. Volunteers may work in direct patient care or in administrative roles. Volunteer assignments are tailored to the needs of the current patient caseload and the personal skills and preferences of the volunteer. Their work may include being a good listener, providing companionship, offering respite care for stressed families, running errands, or just being a caring witness to life's final drama. Volunteers must be sensitive to the needs of others, nonjudgmental about values and beliefs that differ from their own, and willing to spend time with people who are burdened by fatigue, pain, symptoms, and emotional stress due to serious illness.

Dying is not just a medical event. It is a human event. Authentic human contact is the answer to the loneliness and isolation that can occur at the end of life. We as caregivers can approach those at the end of their life as unique individuals, faced with their own life issues that are working themselves out. *When Autumn Comes* poignantly shows that offering this kind of compassionate care is a two-way street.

---

1 National Hospice and Palliative Care Organization, April 18, 2004, Press Release celebrating National Volunteer Week 2004.

2 National Family Caregivers Association. 2000a. 54 million Americans involved in family caregiving last year: double the previously reported figure. Available online at http://www.nfcacares.org/PRSsurvey2000.html (accessed December 2004).

Caregivers often say they get more from the dying than they give to them. One day at a time, the experience of being with someone who is approaching death makes us more grateful for the gift of life.

Les Morgan
President
Growth House, Inc.
www.growthhouse.org
January 2006

INTRODUCTION

During my childhood I grew up in an apartment building in New York City. Our family lived on the sixth floor and my mother's best friend, Helen, lived on the fifteenth floor. As a young child I remember Helen either coming down to our apartment or my mother and I going up to her apartment a couple of afternoons a week. Helen and my mother would have their cocktails while I either listened to their conversations or watched television. I remember Helen's bright-colored wool suits—the prettiest shades of sherbet pink and robin's egg blue. Helen was my godmother; she was always my ally when life seemed too harsh.

In my early teenage years, Helen was diagnosed with cancer. At the end of her illness, she remained at home, where her husband and a private nurse cared for her. Every day my mother collected the soiled laundry and returned it the next morning, clean and folded. This was her gift to her dying friend. Helen's passing was the first time I had lost someone close to me and it opened a Pandora's box of ambivalent feelings about death. As I look back, having now become a companion to the dying as a hospice volunteer, I realize that seeing my mother contribute to Helen's care while she was at home at the end of her life planted a significant seed within me.

Ten years ago, life's mysterious passages led me once again into death's den when my close friend and lover died suddenly of AIDS. The trauma that unfolded in those brief two weeks catapulted me into an entirely new life direction. Recently I came across a book that validates precisely what this experience was like for me. *Crossings: Everyday People, Unexpected Events, and Life-Affirming Change* by Richard Heckler, Ph.D., describes the incredible journey that opens up for us after a catastrophic event. He tells the stories of those who confronted dramatic life-changing events and says that their "desire, to find a context that was big enough to contain their experience, prompted a quest and, unbeknownst to them at first, the beginning of a profound rite of passage."

> Sooner or later it happens to all of us. Something or someone comes hurtling through the trance of our everyday lives and startles us....
>
> What if we consider these events to be signals or messages? What if we attempt to intuit a meaning to the unexpected, or at least acknowledge that something significant has occurred beyond what we ever believed possible? The stories that follow [in Heckler's book] show that when people do so, they cross into a profound and mysterious territory. If they can tolerate the strangeness and inevitable sense of dislocation it engenders, the experience can yield profound treasures—deeper insight, a clearer sense of purpose, and a greater understanding of the world and their place in it (pp. 2, 3-4, 13-14).

One of the blessings of my passage, as I waded through endless days of grief, salvaging a new life for myself, is that death, dying and grief are no longer vague and dreaded silhouettes that haunt me amidst the churning leaves of autumn. At the time, I had no idea just how many bedsides I would occupy offering my companionship. After this sudden and untimely loss, I felt called to pursue training as a hospice volunteer, not only to find purpose beyond my grief but to serve those in this potent time of life.

A hospice volunteer is a humble creature, having no professional status among hospice colleagues. However, since volunteers are not encumbered by an array of specialized tasks to complete during the course of a visit, perhaps this open-ended identity and flexibility, coupled with extended time periods spent with the patient, help lay the foundation for companionship. What I have learned over the years in sitting with the dying is that it is never too late to begin a friendship.

The blessings from such a newly formed friendship run both ways. For the person who is dying, it can be especially healing and validating to have a companion with whom there is no previous history or baggage. The volunteer is able to accept the individual unconditionally, wherever he or she is right now. From this vantage point, the volunteer may be better able to fully attend to the patient and his dying process than family or close friends, whose focus may be divided between the patient's needs and their own issues of grief. Perhaps volunteers provide not only respite for the caregivers but respite for the patient—time away from his inner circle of caregivers, family and friends and the challenging dynamics that can permeate these relationships.

Of the many books I've read and learned from over the years, *Intimate Death* by Marie de Hennezel remains one of my favorite. She summarizes beautifully why caring for the dying can be so rewarding and counters the myth that this work is "depressing."

> I hope to make some contribution to the evolution of our society: toward one that would teach us to integrate death into life, instead of denying it....
>
> I hope to be able to open my readers' minds to the rich rewards that come from being there to share the last living moments of someone close to them....
>
> Even when one enters final helplessness, one can still love and feel loved, and many of the dying, in their last moments, send back a poignant message: Don't pass by life; don't pass by love....
>
> ...I cannot deny the suffering and sometimes the horror that surround death. I've been witness to limitless solitude; I've felt the pain of being unable to share certain times of distress, because there are levels of despair so deep that they cannot be shared.

> But alongside this suffering, I feel I have been enriched, that I've known moments of incomparable humanity and depth....
>
> ...Yes, there was sadness, but there was also sweetness and often infinite tenderness....The space-time continuum of death, for those who accept to enter it and see past the horror, is an unforgettable opportunity to experience true intimacy (pp. xiv, 181-82).

I wrote *When Autumn Comes* to help hospice volunteers and anyone who attends the dying feel more comfortable and confident in this important and rewarding role. If you are a hospice volunteer, are contemplating becoming one, or simply know someone who is terminally ill, you may find yourself pondering the following questions:

How can I step up to the role of being a companion to a dying person? How can I overcome my own awkwardness and fears in approaching someone who is dying? How can I cultivate bonds of trust and intimacy with someone who is preparing for death? How do my beliefs, attitudes, hidden agendas and experiences support or hinder my ability to understand and serve the unique needs of the dying? How can I process and integrate the invaluable lessons about living from individuals who are dying? How do I balance the primary relationship with the person I am visiting with the secondary relationships I have with the caregiver and other family members? How do I reconcile professional boundaries with sometimes strong, personal sentiments toward my patients? And finally, at the end of the day, how does the volunteer or caregiver receive the wisdom and the grace to feel confident that despite any appearances to the contrary, she *does* make a difference in the living and dying of the people she serves?

When Autumn Comes can help you find meaningful answers to these questions. It is my intention through each of the stories I share to give candid and compassionate perspectives about dying from the point of view of someone who is simply a companion to those in the final days of their lives. We are extremely fortunate to have so much literature emerging on the topic of death and dying. It is rare, however, to stumble upon material that is not written by a professional in the field. Hearing the voice of a layperson as she traverses this terrain can, I believe, help expand our collective awareness of the attitudes, beliefs and issues around death, dying and grief—and help us prepare for and cope with our own inevitable journey.

Ultimately, we will all be called to tend to the needs of a loved one who is dying. We will all grapple with the tremendous impact of this grief and loss in our lives and we will all have the opportunity to offer them the compassionate care they deserve. The word *hospice* dates back to medieval times, when it described a house or shelter providing rest and nourishment for pilgrims. In serving the dying, we can all learn to be the open door that welcomes, accepts and comforts travelers making their final journey. It is my prayer that my heart's love and compassion will help ease the suffering and rekindle the wisdom of all who read this book.

Note: Some of the stories I relate are based on my personal experiences with friends or family members. In these instances, I have taken greater liberties in my interactions with the patients and families and may have broached topics that would not be within my role as a hospice volunteer.

1

LOSING A LOVER AND A FRIEND

"Have you heard from James?" the voice at the other end of the phone asked desperately. I had just finished preparing the guest rooms and the laying out of confections for afternoon tea at the bed and breakfast I was managing in Santa Fe, New Mexico. It was the end of my workday and I was planning to walk out the door to renew my driver's license. I never made that trip.

James had taken over my previous job as manager at the restaurant where we had both worked and it was Lisa, the owner, at the other end of the phone. During the past two days, she explained hurriedly, James had not shown up for work and he wasn't answering his phone or returning messages. My relationship with James as a workmate, a lover and now a good friend had been as long, winding and unpredictable as a country road. He was my nemesis and my teacher, a sure-fire catalyst for pain, self-confrontation and transformation. Not returning phone calls was par for the course with James, but not showing up for work sent up red flags for both me and Lisa. I assured Lisa I would stop by his house on my way home and call her when I had some news.

I stood on James' patio outside his apartment for at least 15 minutes, banging away at his door. My knuckles were raw and my heart was pounding as loudly as my knocks. With his car parked right outside and his dog barking away at me, it was obvious James was at home. Why wasn't he answering the door?

Just as I was contemplating calling the police, James finally appeared from the bedroom. "God Almighty," I thought to myself, "when was the last time I saw him? Maybe two weeks ago? How could he have turned into this…this walking shadow of death?" Emaciated, pale and struggling to breathe, James slowly opened the door to let me in. "We're going to the hospital right now," I announced, not mincing words. Neither did he. "No," he replied emphatically.

In between gasps, he told me that a bad cold he had contracted about a month ago had progressed to pneumonia. He took some antibiotics and seemed to recover, but his energy and appetite never bounced back. Within a couple of weeks, he had a relapse. I had seen James twice during this time period. I knew he had been sick, but he never gave me any indication that it was as serious as pneumonia. Since his relapse, James had not sought any medical attention. It became instantly apparent to me that he was just waiting to die and I couldn't grasp why he was not actively seeking help.

I tried every tactic possible to encourage him to let me take him to the hospital. Finally, I threatened to call the police and an ambulance if he wouldn't come with me willingly. Grudgingly, I struck a bargain with him and he with me. James said he needed some time to clean himself up—to bathe, wash his hair and put on clean clothes. Because of his severe oxygen depletion, all these tasks came with tremendous effort and were painstakingly slow. James agreed to come with me to the hospital if I gave him until the next morning to get ready. It was difficult to leave him alone that evening. Fears and dread kept me from getting any rest. The following morning I called James straight away and, true to his word, he was ready to leave when I arrived. Incredibly relieved, I helped him into my car and we raced off to the emergency room. I had such complete faith that the doctors could make James well again.

We did not have to wait to be seen by a nurse. Since nobody was mincing words in this drama, the first question out of her mouth was, "Could you possibly have AIDS?" No pretense with an examination, no pleasantries about the weather, she aimed straight for the jugular. I shot back at her like a cannon, "There's no way—James has been celibate for ages." The nurse ignored me and simply turned to James and asked again, "Could you possibly have AIDS?" Weakly, he nodded yes. I had felt tremors the day before when I took my first good look at James, but now the earthquake hit. There would be many more episodes like this, moments in time when reality was so sharp, intense and poignant that I felt either absolutely raw or absolutely numb.

When I asked the nurse how she figured out he might have AIDS, she said she had seen people come into the hospital over and over again with the same symptoms. They were struggling for oxygen, had pale skin with dark circles under their eyes and had experienced severe and rapid weight loss. Barely holding back my inner fury, I wondered why she just didn't come right out with it—James had death stamped all over him. The nurse ushered us into a cubicle to wait for the doctor on call.

I jumped up onto the examining table and sat right next to James, holding him as he cried. "I'm so sorry," he murmured over and over. "I hope I haven't infected you." He told me that he had probably contracted HIV during his drug-using days, maybe ten years ago. "I never wanted to be tested for HIV," he murmured through the tears, "because I just didn't want to know the results." In the four years I had known James, never had he exhibited any symptoms I would associate with AIDS and yet he seemed as clear about his diagnosis as the ER nurse.

Dr. Levine, a young physician with kind eyes, suddenly appeared. He had a bit more finesse than the nurse or at least was softer around the edges. Dr. Levine immediately ordered oxygen and once that was in place, James said he felt much better. Then the doctor talked to us about blood tests, x-rays and cultures. He wanted to admit James to the hospital so that they could start him on intravenous antibiotics to treat the pneumonia. In the meantime, we would wait for the tests to come back from the lab to determine whether or not James had AIDS.

With that taken care of, my nurturing instincts started to kick in. "Feed him, put some weight on him and he'll get better," I thought to myself. I asked James if he was hungry. When he told me a sandwich and some chips sounded good, I said I would run over to the health food store to pick them up. I held him before I left and told him we would beat this "thing" (AIDS?…Death?…What was this silent enemy we were going after?) "We have to have courage and be strong," I whispered, still holding him, "but we can do it." Then I squeezed his hand, slipped down from the table and left.

As I emerged from the hospital in a daze, I felt totally out of sync with the reality all around me—cars driving alongside me, people shopping casually in the market, the cashier smiling as he rang up my items. "How could they be acting so normal?" I asked myself. In the past 24 hours my entire life had shifted, yet everything around me seemed remarkably untouched and indifferent. I felt like an alien in this "other" world and I longed to get back to the hospital where the characters, props and scenery seemed much more compatible with the life-and-death crisis that was my new world.

We ate our dinner together in his private room. James finished the chips but hardly touched his sandwich. So much for my illusion of nurturing him back to health! Later that evening, a male nurse came to speak to us. Extraordinarily kind, he said he knew that James had just been tentatively diagnosed with AIDS and that we were waiting for the test results. He said he understood how devastating this news must be and wondered if we had any questions or wanted to talk. I don't recall that we had any questions for him or had much to say, but I do remember the courage

> What are some of the coping mechanisms you have relied upon to deal with extreme shock or stress?

and compassion of this kind heart reaching out to us in such a personal and caring way.

He was not afraid to climb down into our dark hole, to acknowledge the immensity of our pain and to offer us his medical knowledge in answer to our questions. He was authentic and totally present with us. I bless this stranger, this angel—wherever he is now. I hope he realized what a precious gift his presence was to me that evening. When he left, I lay down next to James and cried deeply while he stroked my hair. After all my tears were spent and we were both exhausted, I said good-bye and walked out alone into the night.

The next morning, I couldn't wait to get back to the hospital. Maybe some news would be waiting for us. While we were waiting, James asked me to do several chores for him since it seemed he might be in the hospital for a while. He also asked me to help him call his family. His parents were divorced and estranged, his mother living in California and his father in Mexico. His sister and half brother lived in Arizona. James was emphatic about not wanting his family to know that he might have AIDS. Instead, he wanted to refer to his illness as some kind of bacterial respiratory infection that the doctors were still trying to diagnose.

While I disagreed totally with this approach, I told him I would go along with it as long as we could. Soon after speaking with his father, James received a call from a Latino aunt in California. Apparently his father, alarmed by the news that his son was in the hospital, immediately called James' aunt. Practically crying on the phone, she told James she had had a premonition that death was going to strike someone in her family. Not the best of news on either end.

My phone call to James' mother was much less dramatic. Although her brother was also very ill right now and she felt torn about leaving him, when I explained that James' situation was serious she said she would get on the first available flight. After making all the phone calls, James and I were exhausted. "It's all going to change now," he told me. We had woven a tight cocoon around ourselves the past few days. Even in the midst of all this fear and uncertainty, we somehow felt comforted and safe together. The companionship we had known throughout the years of our friendship took on greater significance. James was warning me that once his family arrived, it would be different for us and, in many ways, much more difficult. He was right.

James' father arrived later that day. I returned from dinner to see father and son silently watching the television. Neither had much to say as I entered and it was difficult for me to read how it was going between them. When I asked James if he had heard anything yet about his test results, he barely took his eyes off the television. No, no one had said anything to him. I left the room abruptly to track down James' nurse. Surely the results should have been back by now—it had already been 24 hours. My entire world seemed to rest on those results, but still we had no answers. The nurse had nothing definitive to offer. They were aggressively treating the double pneumonia; that was it for now.

When I returned to James' room to see the same two faces staring vacantly at the television, I lost it. I told them I couldn't believe they were so transfixed by the television and indifferent to the drama unfolding right in front of us. In hindsight I realized that they just couldn't cope with the critical nature of James' condition and that watching TV was a safe outlet for distraction and denial. "Are you mad at me?" James asked contritely after I exploded. I quickly apologized for my outburst, telling him how frustrated I felt at being left in limbo.

James' father pulled me out into the hall and asked me point blank. "What's wrong with James?" I told him what I'm sure James had already explained to him—the story we had agreed on. James had a bacterial respiratory infection and we were waiting for more tests to determine the cause and treatment. All this was true, of course—we just didn't mention the probable diagnosis we were dreading.

During that night at the hospital, James' oxygen saturation began to drop significantly. Although he was still receiving oxygen around the clock with the nasal tubing, it was not enough. When I arrived the next morning, I found him in intensive care, an oxygen mask over his face. He moved back to a regular room later that day, but the oxygen mask remained his constant companion, keeping him comfortable. The mask prevented James from talking, so a notebook and pen became his sole means of communicating from then on. I never heard his voice again.

Family members arrived from California and Arizona daily. James' mother, sister and nephew took up residence in a nearby motel. Of all the many relatives that converged at the hospital during those days, I found the greatest support from being with James' mother and sister. I had met them before this crisis and had established a rapport with each of them. Events like this can often put a terrible strain on relationships, but the three of us somehow held thick and fast.

A recent set of chest x-rays indicated that the antibiotics were not being effective in containing the infection in James' lungs. A stronger combination of drugs was ordered. A low t-cell count and a highly elevated white cell count indicated a severely compromised immune system—another strong indication that James was in the midst of a severe outbreak of AIDS. Although we still didn't have his test results back (tests that should have come back in 24 hours), I had been tested for HIV in the meantime and my results were negative. James was immensely relieved. At least one cloud was no longer hanging over us.

> Why was food such a critical component in how we all tried to care for James?

We knew James would need long-term care if he did indeed have AIDS and I wanted to be his primary caregiver when he was released from the hospital. James agreed to my proposal, but first we had to get him out of the hospital and the pneumonia wasn't abating. I kept falling back to my original line of defense—nutrition. I encouraged James to eat whatever food he could tolerate. Once he asked me to go back to his apartment and prepare a special fortification drink that he had been relying on lately. He dictated the recipe to me—fruit, soymilk and a powdered supplement.

So I started assisting him with his meals, as did members of his family, which helped all of us feel involved. Another night for dinner, James had a craving for a roast beef sandwich from a particular restaurant in town. His father was off in a flash to fulfill this request. James took maybe a couple of bites at the most. I think this probably was his last normal meal.

Finally, a very long five days after James and I walked into the emergency room, the test results came back. His results were quite different from mine. We quietly revisited the issue of telling his family the whole story. I believed that they had pretty much figured it out already. I urged him to be up front now. Besides, keeping such a time bomb under wraps took considerable energy. I was running out of steam, we were running out of time and he was too ill to keep the charade going. Thankfully, he agreed. With the secret out in the open, I knew I would felt much freer.

Dr. Levine explained the situation to the family. James' mother and sister did not seem surprised by the diagnosis, as they were both familiar with James' history of drug use during his youth. But James' father—a proud Latino father and patriarch—did not want to accept this diagnosis or the self-perceived shame it cast upon his son and his family. Overwhelmed by shock and denial, he assumed that James had not yet been told of his condition because in his culture patients simply would not be given that kind of news. Such an admission, James' father felt, would shatter his son's will to live. It seemed to us that James' father was not dealing with the diagnosis and was projecting his need for denial onto James. However, I've learned through subsequent training that individuals or their families deal differently with life-threatening illnesses based on their cultural upbringing and that it is important to be mindful and respectful of these differences when working with patients.

Dr. Levine, however, held firm that he wanted to be entirely candid with James regarding his diagnosis, treatment protocol and prognosis. James was honestly kept abreast of his condition by the hospital staff, who did as well as they could with what little they knew. I believe that James himself probably knew more about his condition than the rest of us since he was the one whose breath was steadily being taken away from him.

Often when we are in the grip of such raw pain in dealing with the death of a loved one, interpersonal dynamics among friends and family become strained. Poor communication skills, power struggles and other dysfunctional relationship patterns can be exacerbated during times of crisis. (I have seen this trend in several of the hospice cases I've been involved with and will explore it further in other chapters of this book.)

Such was the situation between me and James' father—not an easy man to get along with even in the best of times. We seemed to manage together reasonably well at the onset, but as James' conditioned worsened, all attempts at civility between us collapsed under the stress. One evening when James had sent me to his apartment to run an errand, I arrived only to find out that his key didn't work anymore. James' father had changed the locks without telling either of us. When I confronted him, he said that he didn't want anyone going in and stealing James' belongings. What he was really saying was "I don't want you having access to James' home anymore." This was a big blow to me, compounding my grief and stress.

The final standoff with James' father came when he took some photographs of James that I had hung in the hospital room and which belonged to me. When I asked for them back, he told me he was getting copies made because he had no recent pictures of his son. How ironic that his fear that I would steal something from James' apartment was a projection of his own behavior! The next day, he gave me back only one of the two pictures and told me he was keeping the other one. When I spoke with a good friend about the situation, she advised me to let it go. The man was trying to hold onto his son in any way he could. She also reminded me that my love and connection to James was not dependent on any material item. Of course, she was right. James' father had no control over the disease that was rapidly stealing his eldest son from him, so he was exerting control in any way he could.

At times I, too, felt utterly powerless. The suddenness and randomness of James' illness seemed to fly in the face of all that was fair and just in the world. I remember one sunny morning, eating breakfast on the restaurant patio where James and I had worked. James did not want to receive any visitors apart from his family, so I had gone there to give his co-workers a status report. As I was waiting for my food and watching the people walk by, I spotted a particularly fit looking man around the same age as James. I was enraged. Why was he out strutting around in his healthy body while James lay emaciated, struggling for every breath?

To me, this man symbolized many aspects of James that had been lost to his illness. Appalling as it sounds, if I had been a wizard or shaman, I would have cast this illness out of James and sent it into this innocent man. If I had had the power, if I had had any control or say in this situation whatsoever, that's what I would have done. The healthy stranger strolling by epitomized the seeming inequity of this situation and was very hard for me to accept in this stage of my grieving.

On the other hand, I had a firm conviction that God was with us and that whatever happened to James, it was all in His hands. I believed that events were unfolding according to some bigger picture. Although I might not understand all the whys and wherefores at the moment, I trusted implicitly in God's divine order. Having a spiritual center did not preclude me from having to deal with a full spectrum of emotions, particularly grief and loss, but it did give me tremendous strength.

At one point, when James seemed defeated and depressed, I asked for a psychiatrist to evaluate his mental state and will to live. If there was to be any chance for James to rally from this infection, he needed to fight. We were all beginning to see someone who was giving up. None of the rest of us could cope with that yet, although, as I would observe in later years, it is actually common to see this type of withdrawal in someone who is approaching death. The psychiatrist came and visited with James privately for ten minutes or so.

James had now grown physically and psychologically dependent on the oxygen mask and could only tolerate keeping it off for the briefest of moments. When he was without the mask, he would experience such shortness of breath that it felt as if he were suffocating, which would bring on a panic attack, making breathing even more difficult. Since James could not remove his oxygen mask and therefore was not able to speak, he communicated by writing in his notebook. At the completion of his brief interview, the psychiatrist concluded that James was still able to make coherent decisions on his own behalf. According to the psychiatrist, James wanted to live.

His family and I felt encouraged by the evaluation, and the same day I saw a definite shift in James' morale. He asked for a newspaper so he could look at rentals. Studying the classifieds had always been a favorite pastime for him so it was extraordinarily encouraging to see James look to the future. We had already discussed my moving in to care for him upon his release from the hospital, so on his own initiative James started looking in the classifieds for larger accommodations than his one-bedroom apartment. Even if James showed interest in the classifieds simply to comfort me and give me something to hope for, this gesture was tentatively creating a future for us and I clung to this future like a lifeline.

> Could it be possible that James' interest in the classifieds was simply to comfort me, giving me something to hope for?

One night I had tried sleeping beside James at the hospital, but it was a disaster. Besides the problem of the cot itself, the constant activity, noises, lights and other intrusions made any restful sleep impossible. I realized that if I was going to stay sane throughout this ordeal, I had to take reasonable care of myself. Surprisingly, I slept well at home those two weeks. Sleep came as a blessed escape. Still, I often felt torn about leaving James during the night, especially since that was when his crises usually happened.

I arrived one morning to find him hooked up to a ventilator and back in intensive care. After questioning the nurses and James' father (who had stayed the night and was present during the episode), I learned that he had gone into crisis again during the night—unable to catch his breath, low oxygen saturation and unstable vitals. Apparently James pleaded with them to give him more time to try to calm himself and thereby regulate his breathing. The hospital staff, however, felt the ventilator was necessary to keep him alive. In order for James to remain comfortable and relaxed, it became necessary to establish an IV line for a morphine pump. Both the nurses and physician commented to me that despite his initial resistance to the ventilator, James was working well with the machine. He was not agitated or fighting it, as some patients apparently do.

Even with more and more props, James' condition was steadily declining. The antibiotics were ineffective. His mother, sister, Lisa and I were beginning to accept the inevitability of his leaving us. James was mostly sleeping now, awake and coherent only for moments in any given stretch, a common indicator of approaching death. Each of us in turn was telling him that it was okay for him to let go now if that was what he needed to do.

A wonderful nurse came in to do some energy work with James—to help his spirit detach from his body, she said. She placed her hands a few inches above him and slowly began to move them from his feet up to the top of his head. I was comforted by her gentle movements, conveying so much tenderness without ever touching his body. I also set up an altar in the room and played some of James' favorite tapes. We tried to keep the room as peaceful and sacred as possible in the middle of an ICU floor. Technicians were still coming in regularly to draw more blood from James for more tests. Thankfully his mother told them that further tests weren't necessary anymore and asked them to stop.

That afternoon, a social worker called James' father, mother and me into a neighboring empty room in ICU. She said it was easier to talk about these issues before death to help the logistics flow better. She proceeded with the easy questions first. Did we have a funeral home we preferred? No, could she recommend one? Yes, she'd put the name and phone number on James' chart. Next. How did we want his body disposed? I explained that James' religious faith encouraged cremation between 48 and 72 hours after the death. I was not sure how his father would respond to this information. No objection from either parent. We had a brief discussion about where we would scatter the ashes and we tentatively agreed that we could meet somewhere in the future to carry out this task. With this, the meeting ended. I was extremely grateful for the skill and compassion of the social worker, which enabled us to move through this process unscathed.

Early that evening, as the nurse was checking in on James, he wrote her a note. "How long?" he scribbled. It was an honest question. How long would his dying process take? The nurse dismissed him and his need for honesty, chiding him not to think like that. "I've never lost a patient yet on my shift," she pronounced. I knew then and there that James would be the first.

Around eight that evening I was sitting alone with James, transfixed by the machines flashing the numbers of his oxygen saturation and vital signs. The room was dark and silent except for the sounds of the ventilator. All of a sudden, the door flew open and his father led a parade of relatives around James' bed. They called him Jaime and said they were all elated that he had taken a turn for the better. Stunned, I stared again at the flashing numbers. His oxygen level dropped at least ten digits. I was starting to panic, fearing this disturbance was going to push James over the edge. Before I could say anything, his father and family departed as suddenly as they had entered.

> What can be done when the needs of the patient seem to clash with the needs of the family?

I couldn't understand how they could be telling James he was starting to turn around. Perhaps they were cheering him on in the hopes that he would rally with their support. Extremely disturbed by their actions, I went out to the hall to vent my anger at James' nurse for letting such a big group go into his room. In retrospect, I understand that this was another example of the divergent cultural characteristics and personal needs of James' paternal relatives and me. In the midst of traumatic and stressful circumstances, it is not uncommon to see a clash among family members and friends, especially when different ethnic backgrounds are thrown into the mix.

I resumed my vigil in a chair at the foot of James' bed, choosing this position so I could see his full face. Suddenly he opened his eyes and with his hand gestured me to his side. Once there, he stroked my cheek with his hand. With this simple gesture, he was saying he loved me. He was saying goodbye. Gently, I took his hand in mine and put it to my lips. As the tears dripped down, I told him I loved him too. When he fell back to sleep, I left to go home.

During the night, I was awakened by a phone call. I was not startled by this call—I knew it was coming. When I arrived at the hospital, James' mother and sister were already there. All the machines were unplugged and the room was silent. James had died ten minutes ago. The night nurse said he had gone into cardiac arrest as she was cleaning him. She left us alone and closed the door.

Within moments, James' father arrived and we all stood quietly around his bed. The tubes, IVs and wires had been removed. James' mouth was opened in a circle that had been formed around the ventilator. His eyes were closed. His father stepped back as the rest of us tentatively stroked James' head and arms. Nobody cried. The tears would come later. As I looked down upon his lifeless body, it was apparent to me that James' spirit had already gone. I felt detached and indifferent to this shell that was left behind. I think this was my ultimate defense against James' death. Death could claim his body, but his soul could not be touched. I found refuge in the idea that he had been liberated from pain and suffering.

After a while, I dismantled the altar I had set up for him and gathered my belongings as we all prepared to leave. We stood in the corridor for a while talking, and as we were walking towards the elevator, a gurney rolled past us with a sheet covering a body. That was James, I thought to myself. It seemed so strange to see him like that. Again I steeled myself against any sentiment or attachment toward his physical body. From now on I had to learn to love and think of him solely on a spiritual dimension. As I was exiting the hospital, just before dawn, I saw a woman and man approaching the entrance. The woman was in labor, about to give birth and I was struck by the never-ending circle of life and death.

It had been just two weeks since I had received the phone call at work—two weeks of living in some kind of bubble outside of normal, everyday time and reality. The evening I had brought James into the emergency room, I had phoned my employer, explained some of the details of the situation and told her I needed to stay with James through this ordeal. Now I couldn't possibly return to work right away. When I told her my latest news, she was thrown off by the fact that she now had to scramble to find someone to cover for me, but it all seemed far away from me. I never gave my job a second thought after that, even though it was something I loved. The bottom had fallen out of my life and only one thing mattered—James.

James' father, mother and I never did link up to scatter James' ashes. I'm fairly certain James' father had possession of the ashes, but what he ultimately decided to do with them remains a mystery to me. I briefly saw his father several weeks after James died because I had asked him if I could get James' prayer book from him. He showed up one night where I was working to give it to me, along with an enlarged copy of the photograph he had never returned. He never did give me back the original and in the more than ten years that have passed I never heard from him again. In contrast, I have stayed in touch with James' mother, for which I am very grateful.

Despite the flare-ups that arose among us, I could see that it was tremendously healing for James to have his family gathered around him. It was an opportunity for all of us to convey to James how much we loved him. In fact, it may have been the first time that James was really able to receive our love. I certainly witnessed a softening in him as he was more willing and open to receive and express affection. The walls came down—walls of shame, secrecy, unworthiness, isolation.

In the years following his death, I have sometimes wondered whether it was appropriate that I insisted James go to the emergency room. Certainly, when I found him in his apartment, he knew he was dying. Did I override his wishes to die alone in deference to my own sense of panic and fear? Perhaps. Yet I feel that my intervention provided an opportunity for healing and closure for all of us. I also believe that the intimacy we each experienced with James, even in the midst of all the intensive medical procedures to keep him alive, created a comforting environment for James' final passage through life.

While I certainly struggled with grief and loss during the hospital episode, the real work began following James' death. I knew my time in Santa Fe was over and I needed to do something significant to mark the loss in my life. I wanted to re-create my life from scratch. Although most of the professional literature on the subject advises people who are grieving not to make any radical decisions too quickly after the death, this is precisely what I did. I set in motion plans to sell or give away my furniture and most of my other belongings as I prepared to move to a town in Montana that James and I had visited twice before. Prior to James' illness, I applied to take summer courses at a school there, so I thought I might as well make the move permanent.

I was planning to leave Santa Fe in four weeks and needed to earn enough money to get me through my move. What a blessing it was when Lisa stepped up to the plate, asking me to temporarily manage the new dinner shift at the restaurant. Her offer came with a generous salary and the understanding that I would be with her for only one month.

Her offer was a godsend in other ways as well. I would be working with James' old crew—the people who had worked with him every day. It was incredibly healing for me to be surrounded and supported by James' co-workers, to be in a place that James had loved and where he had spent so much of his time. In a niche in the dining room wall, we set up a small memorial altar for James with his picture. I will forever be grateful to Lisa for her wisdom and generosity in creating that space and time for me to heal.

As synchronicity would have it, Dr. Levine came into the restaurant one day. He had no idea that James had worked here or that I was temporarily at the helm. I was so pleased to see him, to be able to thank him personally for all his efforts on James' behalf and to show him the little memorial. He shared with me that James was his first patient ever to die and that his case had impacted him deeply. He said he had prayed for James with the religious community at his synagogue.

These were just a few of the many wonderful opportunities given to me in those early days to express my grief, to receive support and to begin the long journey forward into a new life. I felt truly shepherded by James and his angels. I even composed a poem in preparation for leaving the restaurant. On my last day, I read it aloud and gave copies to my friends and fellow employees.

> Have you put your arms around us
> to hush this shivering grief?
> James, look through the window!
> Do you see us
> huddled around the hearth—our memories of you?
> This blazing fire that holds us steady
> through these empty, aching days without you.

All of us who loved you and are loving you still,
are like brilliant stars of Light.
James, you are our Sun!
You nurture us daily in your radiance—
the golden pure radiance
that beams up our hearts into yours.

As we bustle and burst around this restaurant,
do you pose yourself at the counter,
every now and then, and look on?
Are you still thirsty?
Won't you drink from this pool of tears,
that we may all be healed?

Can you realize the impact
you made on each of us? And how we still struggle
to be glad for your freedom, while trapped inside our loss?
James, we pray for your peace
and our own absolution from sorrow's stain.

It is a hefty mountain we must climb
to meet you beyond the void—
where grief becomes a cloud, thinning into mist,
while melting away…into a joyful burst of Sun!
The Sun that never left us,
but was only hidden by the cloud.

Our beloved James—
We are loving you still.

Embracing a Passion

Ultimately we will all lose someone we love. Understanding the process and reading a book like this can help immensely. It can help us create a comforting environment for those nearing the end of life so they can face death with greater peace and dignity, and it can help us bring greater care and compassion to ourselves and to others in our time of loss.

In the years before my final sojourn with James, I had only experienced the loss of Helen. Following her passing, I had developed an aversion towards death and kept its shadow safely tucked away. I suspect this is how many of us feel about death—a sense of dread that periodically haunts and immobilizes us. My experience with James changed all that. I learned many important lessons, some of which are summarized at the end of this chapter. More importantly, this episode spun me wildly like a dervish until I was re-rooted in a new state, in a new lifestyle (wife and mother), and in a new vocation—as a hospice volunteer.

After a summer of attending classes as I had planned, I spent the remainder of that year finding a job and an apartment, establishing roots in my new community and grieving. It was my nightly ritual to fall into bed exhausted and let the tears flow. I could feel James' presence in the rocking chair across the room. I imagined him silently sitting there, my companion as I cried. I also had a few vivid dreams (which were more like visions) of James and myself. They were tremendously comforting as they rendered his presence so intensely palpable.

Very close to the first anniversary of his passing, while I was working at a restaurant, a customer who bore a striking resemblance to James came in for dinner. My eyes were transfixed on this man and I was overwhelmed. As synchronicity would have it, a male friend of mine also walked into the restaurant while this other man was dining. The overlap of their visits remains striking. The friend would later become my husband.

The following autumn, I participated in a volunteer training sponsored by the local hospice. It had been over a year since James' death. The most difficult work of grieving was behind me and I was eager to glimpse what hospice was all about. At the training, I received an excellent overview of the history of the hospice movement and the two criteria for receiving hospice services: a prognosis by a physician of six months or less life expectancy and the cessation of all curative treatments. We heard from various members of the hospice team—the physician, chaplain, social worker and nurse—as well as several other presentations.

Ready to sign up, I completed the application form, arranged for my letters of reference to be sent to the hospice director and scheduled my interview. I was disappointed, however, to learn during my interview that the hospice program's patient pool consisted mostly of the elderly and served few if any children or young adults. At the time, I felt strongly that I wanted to work with individuals whose deaths would be considered premature, as James' was, so I decided to pursue my own studies of death and dying until I received a clearer sense of how I could serve in this area.

Not long after I got married, and within a few months I became pregnant. With this life ripening inside me, I decided to put aside my studies for a time. I needed to be focusing on gestation, birth and new life, so I shifted gears and happily slid back to the other end of the continuum.

When my daughter turned the corner of her first year, I again felt the calling to care for those nearing the end of life. I decided it was time to put my vocation to the test and I contacted hospice, asking to be put on the active list for volunteer duty. Soon after, I was assigned my first patient. Since that time, I have again and again visited the corridors of death with an increasing sense of awe and comfort.

I've heard it said that it's folly to think that one is able to choose a life's vocation. Rather, the secret code of one's calling in this world is embedded deep within the soul. Our life's experiences, as they grip and mold us, hold the key to decoding this vital information. Taking on the mantle of a vocation is anything but a rational and cognitive process. It is like falling into a well while anxiously awaiting the echo of your soul. It is a surrendering to your passion that sometimes, unbeknownst to you, has been calling out all along. Like peering into a child's kaleidoscope, all the events of your life, when shaken up and twisted around, fall into an amazingly beautiful symmetry—and purpose. Becoming a hospice volunteer evolved into an all-consuming goal for me.

While sitting with James, when time and senses were oddly warped, I offered the only thing I could find—my silence, tears, love and companionship. In those days, I had no idea just how many bedsides I would occupy, offering the same humble gifts. I have come to realize that offering these gifts is precisely what unites all who care for the dying, be they professionals, volunteers, family or friends.

Keys for Creating Compassionate Care for the Dying

Get involved. Family members and friends often want to assist their loved ones in any way they can. Look for opportunities to participate in the patient's care (for example, in feeding, applying cold compresses, adjusting pillows or keeping the mouth clean and moist with a swab).

A single act of compassion goes a long way. Practicing courage and compassion while identifying and empathizing with the needs of the dying and their loved ones can help bridge the chasm of isolation, fear and pain often felt at the end of life. The single visit from the male nurse during James' first night in the hospital was a huge support to both of us.

Respect individual coping mechanisms. Watching television can be a primary coping mechanism for someone with a terminal illness. As with any coping strategy, it needs to be respected. Don't be offended or suggest turning the television off if the patient continues to watch it during your visit—just hope they are watching a decent program!

Encourage activities. Find out what type of hobbies, books, music and pastimes the patient enjoyed. Engaging someone in a focused game of chess or simply handing them the classifieds can be a welcome distraction.

Have patience with family dynamics. In the dying process, when so much is beyond anyone's control, make allowances for patients and family members who are exhibiting controlling behaviors. Maintaining a compassionate, nonjudgmental perspective will convey unconditional love—a healing balm for all.

Communicate concerns. A volunteer or caregiver who has been seeing a patient over a span of time may witness changes in interpersonal dynamics as various family members come to visit. Keep the caregiving team informed of any concerns about the patient resulting from family tensions.

Get standing palliative orders. Respiratory distress can be one of the most terrifying symptoms a patient will face. All patients with respiratory involvement, such as those with CHF/COPD or cancers involving the lungs, should have standing palliative care orders on file to provide symptom relief should it become necessary. When a distressing symptom arises, the caregiver can immediately call the hospice office.

Be sensitive to cultural differences. Over the past decade much progress has been made regarding how honestly and thoroughly a physician should convey news of a terminal diagnosis to the patient. However, in certain cultures being up front and candid can be perceived adversely. If an oncologist were to practice candidness in conveying the diagnosis of a terminal illness to a Chinese patient, for example, it could be received as a death curse, precluding any chance of hope for treatment and possible remission or cure. Be aware of cultural sensitivities.

Learn to pick up signs and signals. It is not unusual for an individual, in the end-stage of a terminal illness, to have a keen, intuitive awareness of how much time he or she actually has left. A volunteer or caregiver may be able to glean some of this information by staying alert for clues and symbols embedded in conversations with the patient. If a patient is requesting to see or speak with someone *today*, waiting until tomorrow to call or to arrange the visit may be too late.

Keys for Self-Care

Cook up a storm. Nurturing the patient through food is a common issue for caregivers. If the wife is providing the care, preparing nutritious meals for her husband may have been one of her primary roles throughout their marriage. When she is suddenly no longer required to carry out this function, she may feel guilty and powerless. Although preparing elaborate meals for the patient may no longer be appropriate, the activity of cooking wholesome food, in smaller portions, can be seen as a coping mechanism and is best supported until it becomes a detriment to the patient's comfort and well being.

Ensure good sleep. Overall withdrawal and sustained periods of sleep throughout the day are typically signs of approaching death. As with newborns, patients' internal clocks may become short-circuited, leaving them awake for long stretches during the night. This can be a particularly lonely and frightening time for the dying. Caregivers, worn out from their daytime duties, should not be expected to keep a vigil with their loved ones at night as well—unless, of course, death is clearly imminent. Medications can be prescribed to help ensure a comfortable night's sleep for both the patient and caregiver.

Seek support. Caregivers need a dependable support system. What may look like an unhealthy relationship to you may be a necessary friendship for the caregiver. Don't pass judgment.

Be aware of natural anxieties. The home environment or place where care is being provided can be like an isolated bubble for the caregiver and the patient. Be sensitive to this fact when you are caring for or are around those providing end-of-life care. Their world has shrunk dramatically and they may have little interest or energy for events outside their immediate surroundings and concerns. In some instances, the caregiver and patient may even feel anxious to venture far from home.

Process stress and grief. It is critical that caregivers and volunteers establish viable support systems to alleviate the accumulation of stress and loss in their lives. Even if the patient, caregiver or family members have strong religious or spiritual backgrounds, they will still need to grieve the losses facing them. Faith does not circumvent grief. Always support the patient, loved ones and yourself in expressing grief. Remember that anger, betrayal and a sense of injustice can all be aspects of the grieving process.

Gain closure in your special way. There are many approaches and preferences in how and when people respond to the loved one's body after death. For some, it is important to spend an interval of private, quiet time with the body before it is removed. On occasion, family members may want to bathe and dress the body themselves. Still others may wish to do all of the above in preparation for keeping the body at home for a 48-hour vigil (see keys in Chapter 10). For me, seeing James' body on the gurney sent the final, definitive message—James was dead. Because of the risk factor of contaminated body fluids, his body was never available for viewing, even for the family.

Take advantage of bereavement services. In compliance with Medicare guidelines, hospice agencies offer free bereavement services to the families of patients for one year after the death of the loved one.

2

FACING DEATH AND DYING

His name was Lars and he was of Scandinavian descent. Lars was in his eighties and had been diagnosed with COPD, chronic obstructive pulmonary disease. I was asked to provide caregiver relief on Sunday mornings while his wife attended church services. His wife Margaret greeted me at the door. In her late eighties, she was no taller than me (4'11") and seemed rather frail as well. I was amazed she was still driving. After Margaret gave me brief instructions for Lars, she negotiated her car out of the garage and was off. Lars was spending most of his days in a recliner and he dozed throughout our visit, as I was told he probably would. Margaret returned in just over an hour. I was relieved that there was nothing I needed to report. My first visit was uneventful and rather than being let down, my confidence felt boosted. I could do this work!

The following Sunday, Lars was much more alert so we took advantage of this opportunity to chat. Lars filled me in about some aspects of his life. He offered me some details of his upbringing in Denmark, his move to the States as a teenager and highlights of his life here in Montana. Lars even offered me a song in the deal,"You are My Sunshine" in Danish! Tired from his tales, he drifted off to sleep, concluding our second visit.

I continued visiting Lars in his home for several more weeks, but problems were beginning to surface. Margaret was having increasing difficulty administering Lars' medication. According to the nurses' reports, she was often over-medicating her husband, forgetting when the last doses were given. If Margaret gave him too much medication, Lars would sleep almost round the clock, unable to be roused for meals or daily routines. Problems also arose with Lars' behavior, symptoms most likely related to his advancing illness. He was becoming belligerent towards Margaret, which in turn was making it increasingly more stressful for Margaret to manage his care at home. And although it was not the optimal outcome for either Lars or Margaret, he was eventually transferred to a nursing home.

I continued my visits with Lars in his room at the nursing home. He was never really happy there and frequently asked for Margaret, though she came to visit him every day. He talked often about wanting to go home while Margaret felt guilty and torn that she was not able to care for him any longer. Their relationship remained strained, as Lars' anger and frustration, over the lack of control over his circumstances, continued to mount. Occasionally, Lars' temper would flare up.

> What are some of the drawbacks of visiting patients who are no longer enrolled in hospice?

By now Lars had been receiving hospice care for six months. The team determined that his condition had stabilized sufficiently to no longer warrant our services. After Lars had been discharged from hospice, I had been told that I could continue to visit him on a personal basis, but not in the capacity of a volunteer.

Lars had several falls while trying to get from his bed to the bathroom. With each visit, I'd see more bruises on his body. During one of my visits, Margaret tripped over Lars' oxygen tubing and gashed her head badly. I wondered if these falls were happening, at least in part, because of the pent-up emotions that were festering between the couple. Lars celebrated his birthday and Christmas inside the nursing home, and these were happy occasions as friends and family gathered round him.

Then between Christmas and New Year's a rapid and sharp decline began. Lars stopped eating and drinking, spent most of the time sleeping and became increasingly less responsive. Margaret witnessed these changes in her husband and felt confused and distraught. Because of Lars repeated falls, Margaret was not very confident in the care he was receiving. She was considering moving him to a different facility. Due to his rapid decline, Margaret was also wondering when she should call his relatives and ask them to come. Seeing how agitated she was, I suggested that she speak with Lars' nurse, and I offered to join her in that conversation. The nurse appeared very stressed and seemed immediately defensive toward Margaret's questioning. Without much compassion (or so it appeared to me), she simply explained that Lars was actively dying and they were trying to keep him as comfortable as possible. She saw no point in moving Lars unless Margaret wanted to take aggressive measures to prolong his life in the hospital. As for contacting his relatives, she could not offer any advice, as there was no way of knowing for sure when Lars would actually die. My impression from that conversation was the overall inability of the nurse to validate Margaret's concerns or to support her through a very painful ordeal. At one point the nurse asked if I was a relative and I explained that I was a hospice volunteer.

The day after this conversation, I received a phone call from my supervisor, the hospice volunteer coordinator. Apparently the hospice director had just received an irate call from this nurse complaining about me and my interference in Lars' care, referring to this meeting with Margaret. It was clear that I had erred in identifying myself to the nurse as a hospice volunteer.3 In retrospect I realized I did so in order to have greater clout on Margaret's behalf. Good intentions aside, I understood that what I did was wrong and so I apologized to my supervisor. I explained my version of the details of the meeting with the nurse, Margaret and myself. My supervisor could then see the bigger picture and thankfully the incident passed without further repercussion.

After the meeting with Lars' nurse, Margaret decided to keep Lars where he was, but also decided it was time to call his family. With Margaret and other close family around his bedside, Lars died peacefully in the night.

This dynamic between Lars and Margaret marked the first of several instances where I wondered whether or not our hospice team had somehow come up short in addressing the needs of our patients and their families. Unresolved family tensions, stressful care-giving demands, financial concerns, ineffective symptom control and pain relief, and lack of optimal and comprehensive care facilities for the dying all contribute to scenarios that are less than ideal in caring for the terminally ill. But how much control do we really have over some of these factors? How involved can our team become in difficult family dynamics—patterns that have developed over the course of a lifetime? How are physical symptoms and unmanageable pain exacerbated by a person's beliefs, expectations and attitudes? And when there is no residential facility designed solely for the needs of the dying, how can we offer patients optimal choices for care, when care at home is no longer feasible? These questions reflect the existential angst I've struggled with, as I've witnessed these issues surface periodically among patients I've served. When I am dealing with concerns or questions regarding a patient's care, I've never hesitated to discuss the situation either privately with a staff member or to bring it up during the IDT meeting. (IDT stands for the inter-disciplinary team of hospice professionals who meet weekly to review each patient's current symptoms and plan of care. Volunteers are invited to attend these sessions if they have been assigned a patient.) I may not always understand the team's decision, especially since it is quite possible that I am not privy to all the deter-

How does the volunteer come to terms with the unresolved suffering of a patient or their family?

mining facts because of patient confidentiality. But I do appreciate that my input is always encouraged and weighed in the decision making process.

Regardless of all the factors that are beyond our control to cure, starting with the very disease itself, there are many areas where we can make a positive and potent difference. It is important to note that all hospice programs accredited by Medicare, both non-profit and for profit agencies, are mandated to utilize volunteers as part of the services offered to hospice patients. Whether it is respite relief for the primary caregiver or driving someone to a doctor's appointment, hospice volunteers provide valuable backup and support for the terminally ill and their families.

Some basic skills that will assist volunteers in their work with the dying are naturally emphasized during hospice training. Many volunteers share the experience of having actively participated in and grieved the death of a loved one. However, if you've ever wondered about how death is hidden away in our culture; if you've ever noticed that the subject of death and dying is not the most talked about topic at your cocktail parties; if you ever considered the possible circumstances around your own dying and how you would define a "good death" for yourself or your loved ones; or if you would just like to have more information and understanding about topics related to death and dying, then signing up for a hospice volunteer training course wouldn't be such a bad idea.

I think many of us have vague and sketchy notions about death in general. But if you ask someone how they would feel if a loved one was dying, or how intimate and available they could be with someone in the throes of death, he might draw a blank. Often people simply aren't paying much attention to their deep-seated feelings—or fears—about death. It's one of those areas in life that, as a society, we tend to avoid until it lands on our doorstep. But sooner or later, death does pay us a visit, either directly or via someone we love; and if we haven't spent much time beforehand considering our feelings toward death, we may find ourselves overwhelmed and unprepared to deal with the bombardment of emotions, details and decisions we are faced with. So, taking a volunteer training course, signing up for an adult education class or simply borrowing available books from the library may be the first step towards illuminating and exploring the foreboding caverns of death and dying. But like going through a loved one's death, completing a volunteer training program does not guarantee that you are volunteer material or that you even want to be!

Among the myriad of skills and attributes that serve as reliable tools for working with the dying, the single most important skill is active listening. Active listening means being fully present and attentive to the person who is talking to you. Rather than being distracted by your own inner dialogue, you, as a listener, are entirely available to the thoughts and feelings of the person who is sharing with you. In this capacity, you are able to convey to the other person a profound sense of caring and respect. Without having to say a word or do absolutely anything, your ability to attend becomes a tremendous gift. It is a gift that, if offered sincerely and consistently, is a key component in becoming a companion to the dying.

Most of our friendships are typically not hindered by the same time constraints that impact our friendships with people who are terminally ill. Grains left in the hourglass are swiftly diminishing before our eyes and we just can't count on an infinite number of tomorrows to get acquainted with each other. Actively listening to someone, instead of poking your own thoughts into a conversation, creates an open doorway to the heart and soul of that person. It gives you more understanding about who they are and where they've come from. It gives you the ability to better perceive their current needs and perhaps also their most present fears. Basically, being a good listener gives you vital information and this information can in turn greatly impact the quality of care you and the hospice team are able to provide. It is a crucial component in getting to better know the individual and what physical, emotional, mental and spiritual challenges they may be experiencing.

There is no substitute for active listening. It's not something easily fudged, especially with the dying. If they are conscious, they will know if you are being authentic or not. So if your desire is truly to be a companion for the dying, this is where it all begins and ends.

Key for Creating Compassionate Care for the Dying

Keep your ears open. Active listening is the most valuable skill a companion to the dying can offer. Rather than being distracted by our own inner dialogue, we are simply listeners, fully present and attentive to the thoughts and feelings of the person sharing with us. Being unconditionally available to someone in this way conveys a profound sense of caring and respect. When offered sincerely and consistently, this tool is a tremendous gift to the dying.

Keys for Self-Care

SOS: Call for help. Caregivers and volunteers are sometimes faced with difficult issues and with questionable outcomes during their sojourn with a loved one or patient. Self-care in these stressful situations is crucial. Many hospitals sponsor caregiver support groups. As a first step in getting the help you need and answering your questions, ask your oncologist or hospital social worker for a referral to a support group or contact the hospice social worker. Likewise, volunteers can contact their coordinator.

Keys for Hospice Volunteers

Watch for changes. Hospices often feel pressure from regulatory agencies to discharge patients after six months of service. To justify ongoing hospice care, the hospice team must carefully weigh the current history of patients for evidence of sustained and overall decline in their condition. Occasionally, individuals released from hospice will take a sudden turn for the worse, dying shortly after they are discharged. Patients who have been discharged can once again qualify for receiving hospice services if their condition deteriorates significantly.

Maintain professional boundaries. My hospice agency has recently instated new guidelines for volunteers that prohibit personal involvement with patients or their families immediately following the patient's discharge or death. Maintaining appropriate, professional boundaries is essential for protecting both the clients and the volunteers. Forming emotional attachments with patients or family members can lead to unhealthy dependencies. As in any therapeutic setting, there must be clear, defined roles between the patient and the professional.

Don't misrepresent yourself. In situations where you are not acting in your capacity as a hospice volunteer, don't use your hospice affiliation in an inappropriate manner. By overstepping proper boundaries, I inadvertently created friction between the nurse and the hospice agency I was representing and I learned a valuable lesson.

3

SOMEWHERE BETWEEN FEISTY AND ORNERY

Sedona was an elderly woman dying of congestive heart failure. Her grandson, Stan, was caring for her in his home. This was an extended family setting including a wife (who had no responsibility for Sedona's care), children, in-laws, grandchildren, even cats and canaries. The environment was not always warm and harmonious, however, and sometimes when I came to visit the stress was palpable. Although Grandma was supposedly hard of hearing, she was quite savvy to the household dynamics and would typically fill me in on the latest argument or upheaval. It took me a while to sort out all the characters in the drama and who was related to whom, but slowly I pieced it together with Sedona's help.

In a way I think she enjoyed the commotion around her—perhaps it gave her something to think about. It certainly gave her something to talk about, with me anyway. Sedona's room was immediately to the left as you came into the front door of the house, so she really was right in the thick of things. Family members would occasionally come into her room and visit. Sedona especially enjoyed the youngest child, a rambunctious one year old. He'd come up to the gate that was used specifically to keep him out of Sedona's room and peek his head around. He didn't shy away from Grandma as some of the others did. That little boy was able to accept Grandma on her terms and this suited both of them just fine.

Feisty with a propensity towards ornery is a fair description of Sedona's personality. I was told that my predecessor (the first volunteer) was 'fired' because Sedona found her a nuisance. I confided with Stan that I hoped I would be more to her liking. And I guess I was—I got to visit twice a week.

Sedona had plenty of stories to tell about her life in Montana, which I thoroughly enjoyed hearing. I asked her if she'd mind if I brought along a tape recorder the next time I visited so we could record some of her stories. (A "life review" can be an extremely valuable exercise for someone preparing for death. Seeking a sense of meaning and closure to one's life, engaging in such a review can help an individual zero in on particular experiences that gave their life purpose and direction. In order to provide this opportunity to their patients, many hospices offer specific training to their staff and volunteers in facilitating a life review). Sedona didn't seem to care one way or another about my suggestion, so being an optimist, I took that as a yes and I came prepared next week to record. Well, if she didn't have an opinion before, she certainly had one now! Sedona wasn't going to say another word until I got rid of that dang blasted thing. And she pursed her lips together and stared straight ahead. No amount of my coaxing or explaining would convince her to speak into my little black box. So, I gave in and tucked it away in my hospice sack (along with the disposable gloves, face mask and disinfectant soap, in compliance with universal precautions). Sedona smirked triumphantly, or maybe it just seemed so.

> Can you identify instances in this story where Sedona was able to exert a healthy sense of control over her situation?

What I didn't get to record for her family, I did get to hear for myself. During one episode, Sedona suddenly broke into tears. She had been reminiscing about her children and it seemed as if suddenly and quite unexpectedly she was drawn into a vortex of grief. When I gently asked her what was the matter, Sedona explained that she had lost a child at an early age due to illness and an adult son in a logging accident. These losses were in addition to the deaths of her husband and parents, and the expression of her compounded grief was sharp and painful. When the death of a loved one is not fully grieved, with any subsequent deaths the grief is compounded and can take a serious toll—physically, psychologically and/or emotionally—on the individual. Receiving adequate grief support for any significant loss, be it pet or person, is imperative.

Sedona continued her story, relaying that she had prayed to God to spare her young child and when He didn't, she turned away from God in anger and pain. Sedona also shared in a different conversation that she had subsequently taught Sunday school classes for the children in her church community. It was enough for Sedona to allow her grief to surface again—that was as far as she was willing to go with it. And I respected her wishes.

Sedona had declined a visit by the hospice spiritual care coordinator, instead receiving periodic visits from her grandson's minister. From what I could gather, Sedona treated him cordially, but it didn't seem like anything of great depth was explored or shared. Apparently Sedona was not interested in changing her mind about God at this late stage of the game.

One day I asked her if she thought she might see her children again. She seemed confused, but interested and asked me what I meant. I explained that some people, as they draw closer to dying, receive visits from their loved ones who have already crossed over. Sedona didn't embrace the idea, nor did she dismiss it. Being as feisty as she was, I went on to suggest that she keep her eyes and ears open for some unexpected visitors!

Sedona's decline was gauged by her mobility to a chair. Before I started visiting her, Sedona was able to get herself out to a chair in the living room using her walker for assistance. During my involvement with her, she was at first still able to get from her bed to a nearby recliner in her bedroom, and this is where I would usually find her when I arrived. As the weeks wore on, getting out of bed unassisted was no longer a safe option for Sedona, but trying to convince her of this was another story! The commode was placed next to her bed for bowel movements although Sedona also typically wore briefs, just in case. After a few nights of Sedona trying to get to the commode by herself and falling, guardrails were installed on her hospital bed. But this didn't slow her down; she then learned to crawl down to the end of the bed, past the rails, to gain her freedom. Stan slept with a baby monitor by his bed so he would awaken when he heard any stirring in Grandma's room. When he'd go into her room to check, she typically needed to use the commode. Grandma had the urge to pee and could not get used to the catheter. One night Stan found her at the bottom edge of her bed with her catheter tubing somehow knotted up around the bed railing.

> Were the guardrails more of a hindrance or a help in ensuring Sedona's safety?

Sedona's nightly antics were wearing out her grandson. In addition to trying to get out of bed, her thinking was becoming more and more disoriented. At times, she feared she was being poisoned and refused to eat. On other occasions, she seemed to lose touch with the present and reverted back to episodes from her past, as if they were currently happening. Even situations that had happened to her husband during the war seemed to be playing out for Sedona in the present. It was very difficult for Stan to communicate with and to reassure her during these episodes. Sedatives were prescribed, as well as medication for her increasing anxiety, but little improvement was seen. Typically, Sedona would be up all night, finally dropping off at four a.m., and sleeping most of the following day. Stan could no longer cope with this exhausting schedule, but declined the suggestion of hiring someone to sit with

Sedona at night, because he feared it would too quickly deplete his grandma's already limited financial resources.

A four-day holiday weekend was approaching and additional family members were coming to visit. The social worker from hospice suggested that Sedona go into the hospice room at the hospital to give her family some respite time together. Sedona did not want to be moved to the hospital and did not hesitate to say so. Stan was obviously struggling with the situation. Worn out from too little sleep and the caregiving demands of his grandma, coupled with the need of other family members to enjoy a weekend without Grandma, Stan decided to place her in the hospital.

This is an excellent example of the dilemma that is sometimes faced in balancing a patient's needs and desires with the needs of their caregiver and family. Clearly, Sedona did not want to be moved from her grandson's home. However the quality of her care was being compromised by Stan's mounting stress. As frustrating as it was for me to accept the transfer to the hospital, without backup support for Stan, I understood it was no longer a realistic or safe alternative to keep Sedona at home.

Sedona was very disoriented her first day in the hospital. She didn't know where she was and felt very agitated. The nursing staff was finally able to calm her and her second day passed much more peacefully as Sedona slipped into a coma. She died the following day, alone.

Is this the death Sedona had wanted all along and maybe didn't realize it? In the hospital, she was able to have some peace and quiet, and rest. Perhaps all the comings and goings at Stan's home prevented Grandma from truly relaxing and letting go. From all accounts, Sedona died peacefully. Could she have found that same serenity at home? These are questions we may never be able to answer with certainty. But what we can say about all those who cared for Sedona is that we did the best we could in honoring her wishes, while recognizing the needs of her family as well.

Do you think Sedona had a good death?

Keys for Creating Compassionate Care for the Dying

Encourage a life review. Though not restricted to those facing imminent death, a life review is a common and valuable tool for those actively engaged in the dying process. A life review enables an individual to step back and take a wide-angle look at his life by talking about his triumphs and defeats, his relationships, his strengths and shortcomings—everything that contributed to who he is. Undertaking this inventory with the support of friends and family is a great opportunity for reconciliation, healing and forgiveness, for oneself and for others. We should not push anyone into a life review, but we can help the process unfold naturally by asking key questions at the right time. To provide patients with this opportunity, many hospices offer training to staff and volunteers in how to facilitate a life review.

Test the waters gently. When conversing with those in the final stages of their life, we walk a fine line between unconditionally accepting what they are saying and breaking into difficult territory by asking them to confront their pain. In this case, Sedona's decision not to tape record stories about her life as a gift to her family was clear and final and it was appropriate to honor her request.

Accept their reality. Don't dismiss accounts of conversations between dying patients and their deceased loved ones as mere hallucinations resulting from overmedication. Instead, consider this a natural phenomenon of the dying process. These experiences are entirely real to the patient and we must accept that reality as a part of their experience. *Final Gifts: Understanding the Special Awareness, Needs and Communications of the Dying* (listed in Appendix B, "Selected Readings") is an excellent resource on this topic.

To pee or not to pee. There are a number of areas where we must balance the needs of the dying with the needs of those who are caring for them. One involves an ongoing debate over the use of catheters for the dying. Those opposed argue that catheters are often used simply for the convenience of the nurses, especially in nursing home settings, at the expense of the patient's comfort. Proponents counter that when a patient can no longer manage a commode, catheters help prevent skin breakdown from urine and ease the burden on caregivers. When addressing this issue, carefully weigh the caregiver's needs with the patient's needs.

Trace the source of anxiety. When medications are not effective in mitigating anxiety, patients could be experiencing a spiritual crisis. Asking their permission to contact their minister or the hospice's spiritual care coordinator on their behalf may be helpful. In Sedona's case, grief over the loss of her children and her subsequent ambivalence toward God may have been indicators of a spiritual crisis that was not being addressed by the occasional visits of her minister. Since she refused a visit from the hospice spiritual care coordinator, however, the team could not explore this possibility with her. Stay open to the need to provide spiritual support.

Keys for Hospice Volunteers

Keep those gloves on. For health and safety, hospice volunteers should be thoroughly trained in and feel comfortable using universal precautions (standard hygienic barriers, such as disposable gloves and face masks, that prevent the spread of infectious diseases).

It's our job to serve, not to save. Hospice does not represent or promote any one religious affiliation or agenda. The spiritual care coordinator for hospice supports individuals and families in finding comfort and peace within their own religious or spiritual framework. In comforting the dying, there is a marked difference between drawing on one's spirituality for inner strength and imposing one's religious beliefs.

If a volunteer feels the need to introduce his own belief system to patients, he may not be an appropriate candidate for hospice work. Pastoral care training within his own religious community would probably be a better choice for such volunteers.

Write it down. The hospice team gauges a patient's decline by a number of factors, including changes in the patient's mobility. Be sure to note any deterioration in the individual's condition and to share this information with the team. This documentation is critical for qualifying the patient for a renewal of hospice services after the six-month mark.

Don't take sides. Should hospice volunteers advocate for the patient or for the caregiver? Often the answer is not easy or obvious. Carefully consider both perspectives, using all the information available. Strive for a win/win situation, but be realistic about the limitations involved and work with them accordingly.

Maintain confidentiality. Patients often confide in volunteers and we must honor that relationship of trust. If certain information seems critical to the individual's care, it is appropriate to share this at interdisciplinary team meetings, where hospice professionals and volunteers meet to plan care for patients. However, even within the context of these meetings discuss only the details that are relevant to the patient's overall care plan.

4

HEALTHY BOUNDARIES

I never met Eileen personally. Aspects of her case were shared with the volunteers as part of an in-service training on maintaining professional boundaries while working with the dying.

Eileen was an 84-year-old widow with breast cancer. She had two adult daughters residing in other states and lived alone in a condo she bought after her husband died. Eileen was a sweet and gentle soul whom, those assigned to her care, looked forward to seeing. It was rather unusual to have a patient who was so endearing and was able to give you far more than you were ever able to give to her. Volunteers were assigned to help with groceries, meals and light house cleaning; home health aides came in three times a week for bathing; nurses closely monitored any uncomfortable symptoms or pain. Eileen's care initially was well managed and she was very enamored with the hospice team, as of course they were with her!

Then, without anyone at first really noticing, things began to change. As the disease process started to gallop, her overall needs steadily inched their way up the scale. With no primary caregiver, individuals on the hospice team gave Eileen their home phone numbers in case she should need any extra help. Normally, home numbers were never given out to clients, but the staff and volunteers wanted to make an exception for Eileen. She was so kind and appreciative of everyone's help that people just wanted to do everything they could for her. The team also knew how important it was for Eileen to maintain her independence and to remain in her own home.

This understanding, coupled with her warm and generous spirit, were the key motivators behind people's willingness to do those little extras to keep her comfortable. What hospice didn't bargain for was that because Eileen's condition was inevitably deteriorating, members of the team each had to do more and more for her to be able to remain at home. And sometimes Eileen unintentionally put people in difficult positions. For example, if the home health aide noticed bruises and asked her about them, Eileen would respond that she had taken a couple of spills. She would then ask the aide not to bother mentioning it to the nurses, as it was really nothing serious. So what does the aide do with this information?

> How does this story illustrate the interpersonal dynamics of hospice team?

Everyone was emotionally invested in their relationships with Eileen, and although no one initially could put their finger on the problem, it was obvious that something was going wrong. One person said that all of a sudden she felt as if she were drowning in this situation and didn't know how to pull herself out. It was finally during a team meeting, specifically called to address Eileen's case, that everyone was able to give voice to their ambivalent feelings regarding Eileen and her care. The manager of the hospice (whose role does not typically entail direct patient care but rather overseeing the care from a clinical perspective) was able to help the group identify how each one of them had gone down the proverbial slippery slope in caring for Eileen. The team's collective desire to go out of their way in taking care of Eileen had actually done her, and themselves, a serious disservice. By overlooking various professional codes of conduct, they had unintentionally set up an unrealistic scenario for Eileen, one that was becoming increasingly impossible for them to sustain. The team was enabling her to stay at home, when it really was no longer in her best interest to do so without receiving supplemental support, either from a family member or from a privately paid health aide. In Eileen's documented plan of care, there were x number of hours allotted for care in specific areas, when in fact, the care she was actually receiving from various team members, off the record, far exceeded these hours.

Brainstorming the problem thoroughly, it was decided that certain professional boundaries needed to be put back in place and her plan of care needed to be restricted to only what was prescribed during the interdisciplinary team meetings. Initially, this solution was very difficult for Eileen to accept. Understandably, she ended up feeling that hospice was abandoning her. However, shortly after these changes had been put in place, she experienced a crisis that necessitated a brief hospitalization. Her stay in the hospital precipitated a response from one of her daughters, who then decided to return home to care for her mother. As a result of her daughter's care, Eileen was able to remain at home until she died a few months later.

Eileen's story illustrates how easy it can be for us to miss the mark in serving the needs of our patients, how complicated it can be to uphold professional boundaries amidst intense emotional feelings, and how critical it is to maintain honest and open lines of communication with our teammates in order to better assess the motives, actions and the overall care of those we are serving.

Keys for Hospice Volunteers

Maintain healthy boundaries. When we become emotionally over invested in a relationship with a patient, it is easy to overstep boundaries, which could compromise their best interests. To prevent this from happening, be sure to openly and honestly communicate with your hospice team. It is common for hospice supervisors to ask potential volunteers about this topic during the interview process to access their understanding and ability to uphold this professional standard.

5

IT'S THE EYES THAT DO THE TALKING

My first memory of Lucia is from the day before my wedding. Lucia was a member of my church community, and although I frequently saw her at different church services and functions, I had never really gotten to know her. My wedding was going to be celebrated in our recently remodeled sanctuary. In fact, it was to be the first ritual conducted inside those newly spiffed-up walls, just one day after the dedication ceremony. Lucia approached me at the conclusion of the dedication service and assured me that she would be at church the following morning, "praying up the sanctuary" before the wedding was to begin. I was deeply touched by her gift of thoughtfulness and prayer.

My friendship with Lucia continued to deepen over the years. She had moved to this country from Holland several years prior to our meeting and still retained many delightful characteristics from her homeland. From her traditional woolen jackets to her wooden clogs, from her thick Dutch accent to her sparkling eyes and rosy cheeks, Lucia exuded a spry spirit that was joyful, playful and altogether embracing.

As I was awaiting the birth of my first child, Lucia intercepted me one day at church and handed me a notebook. It was full of beautiful pictures of nature, art and babies! One picture in particular, of an infant's face, captivated me. Lucia explained that she had compiled this notebook for her own daughter when she was pregnant and that it was very important for women to focus on beautiful, uplifting images during their pregnancies. Again, I was grateful for her thoughtfulness and browsed through the book regularly. I had been looking for a visual image of how I imagined my baby would look and the infant's face in the notebook was an ideal representation. Sure enough, when my daughter was born, she looked very similar to that picture!

One Thanksgiving, Lucia and I were sharing dinner with our church community. I noticed that something was not quite right about her. She seemed more quiet and withdrawn than usual. She was not sparkling. It was difficult to converse with her because her voice was low and she seemed to be mumbling rather than talking. I also noticed that her leg seemed to be involuntarily shaking.

Several weeks later, right after Christmas, the minister made an announcement at church that Lucia was ill and was considering going back to Holland. I was shocked and immediately phoned her when I got home. I couldn't understand her over the phone, since her voice was low and mumbling, so I said I would be right over. I was incredulous when she opened the door to her home. Her appearance and dress were usually immaculate, but today she wore old clothes and her hair wasn't brushed. The light was gone from her eyes, and at first, I wasn't even sure if she recognized me—I barely recognized her! I sat down very close to her and concentrated intently as she spoke, trying to piece together her story. Her voice again was low and muffled. This coupled with her Dutch accent made it difficult to catch everything she was saying. Lucia also seemed to be having a hard time finding the words she needed to convey her thoughts. Fluent in English and articulate, Lucia typically conversed with ease. But today language was a stranger to her; she did the best she could to summon the right words. This is how I understood her situation.

The previous summer Lucia had returned to Holland to visit family and friends for several weeks. Around October, Lucia wasn't feeling well. Her energy level and appetite were down significantly, she started experiencing some forgetfulness and general disorientation, she was having difficulty sleeping at night and was experiencing unusual tingling sensations in her arm. As we were talking, I noticed that Lucia's left leg shook constantly and involuntarily. As the weeks progressed, she explained that she could not continue on with her various cleaning jobs, as she would misplace the keys to get in or forget where she was. Driving was no longer safe because she was so disoriented. Lucia believed strongly in alternative medicine and diet. She had studied herbs, homeopathy, yoga and nutrition. Years earlier, she had cured herself of cancer through holistic medicine. Initially she applied what she knew toward her own self-treatment, but the symptoms continued to worsen. Lucia feared that whatever was going on with her could be very serious.

Lucia had two adult daughters who lived nearby. The day I had come to visit, she explained that her daughters were in the process of booking a flight for her back to Holland. Her reason for wanting to return was that she could receive medical treatment at a nominal cost due to the country's socialized healthcare system. Lucia was very clear on this point—she did not want to become a burden (financial, physical, emotional or otherwise) to her daughters.

I was stunned by everything I was hearing. I had seen Lucia just a month ago and had no idea that any of this was going on for her. I also felt very concerned about her decision to leave the country. I knew she had some family over there, but would they be in a position to care for her to the extent that she would need? In her present confused and debilitated state, I envisioned such a journey as being extremely taxing and most likely further jeopardizing her already precarious health. I asked Lucia, if money and ample support were not issues, would she choose to stay home. Her answer was yes. I made a promise that I would help her through this—that whatever it took, I would stay with her. As I was leaving, Lucia showed me two egg cartons full of her gorgeous hand-painted Ukrainian eggs. She asked me if I would try to sell them for her at our church. I told her I'd be happy to. As it turned out, her daughters asked that I return the eggs to Lucia; they wanted them for keepsakes. Nevertheless, her placing these precious and very fragile eggs into my hands had a very symbolic meaning for me. As I look back on everything that transpired in the few brief months that followed, I believe that in offering me those eggs (a spiritual symbol of death and rebirth) Lucia may have known on some level that she was preparing for her death and was asking me to walk this journey by her side. My impression was that the exchange of eggs symbolized this covenant between us.

Hoping that I could convey to each of the daughters Lucia's desire to remain in Montana, I immediately put in a phone call to her eldest daughter, Caroline. I explained that Medicaid would most likely be available for Lucia if she didn't have any of her own resources to cover future medical expenses. Caroline shared that she and her sister, Lena, both wanted their mother to stay put, while they tried to figure out what on earth was going on with her. Caroline had consulted with a family friend and holistic practitioner and they were tossing around some ideas. Lucia was scheduled to see a physician and have some blood work done, in the hope that this would provide some clues. Both daughters were thinking that a tick might have bitten Lucia and perhaps these strange symptoms were the onset of Lyme's disease. At any rate, they agreed that it was best to keep her here, at least until they had a firm diagnosis. Caroline told me she'd call me when any news came in.

I went to visit Lucia the following week and saw that her belongings were being packed up. She explained that she was going to live with Caroline. Lucia seemed depressed and withdrawn. I didn't stay long since she was expecting another visitor. She also said she was tired and wanted to rest. I called Caroline and she told me that nothing had turned up from the lab tests. The physician who examined Lucia ruled out Lyme's disease, as this was one of the tests that had come back negative. Since Lucia's meager savings had all but run out, there was not enough money for the rent on Lucia's home, so Caroline suggested that her mother move in with her.

This arrangement lasted only a short while because Lucia's confusion and disorientation continued to worsen dramatically. She would wander off from the apartment and go into neighbors' homes not knowing where she was. She rearranged the kitchen cupboards with bathroom supplies. She would frequently leave the stove on unattended. Clearly Lucia needed more constant supervision than Caroline could provide for her. She was showing signs of advanced dementia, which could not be attributed to any known cause. The daughters decided to place Lucia in a nursing home, so that she could receive round-the-clock care and supervision, while the hunt for a diagnosis continued. Caroline had contacted someone with social services who was helping the daughters complete the paperwork necessary for Lucia to receive disability and Medicaid benefits.

I went to see Lucia her first day at the nursing home and what I saw left me in total shock and grief. It was probably a week, maybe two, since I had seen her last and her deterioration in that brief window was unbelievable. She could no longer communicate intelligibly. Lucia would mumble in what sounded like another language. When I later asked Caroline if she was speaking Dutch, she said that it sounded like Dutch, but for the most part it was unintelligible. She used some words here and there, but nothing that would constitute a coherent train of thought. When Lucia sat in a chair or walked, her head was bowed low in front of her. She seemed to recognize me, but did not know my name. For the most part, all Lucia did now was wander through the corridors of the nursing home, looking very much like someone with Alzheimer's disease. We knew that was not what we were

> When you see a patient decline so rapidly from one visit to the next, how do you process feelings of shock, concern and loss without burdening the patient?

dealing with, however, because of the sudden onset and rapid progression of her symptoms.

Within a few days of her arrival at the nursing home, Lucia developed some kind of infection. Running a very high fever, she was taken to the hospital and admitted for some further tests. At this juncture a neurologist performed a thorough evaluation; finally we were on a course toward diagnosis. The neurologist assigned to the case was initially just as baffled as we were. Clearly, Lucia's dementia was progressing. The round of tests the doctor ordered did not indicate anything definitive and, without an invasive brain biopsy, we would never have a conclusive diagnosis. But the physician did suspect a fairly uncommon disease, known as hereditary Creutzfeldt Jakob disease or CJD, the human derivative of mad cow disease. A rare, incurable and degenerative brain disorder, CJD would eventually lead to severe dementia, coma and immune system failure. It seems that the neurologist had studied under a physician named Stanley Prusiner, who was renowned in the field for his research of this particular disease. As uncommon as CJD was, Lucia's physician had had some exposure to it. To date, there are only about 250 cases reported each year. Since transmission of this disease is predominantly hereditary, the neurologist asked the daughters to please contact Lucia's family members in Europe to see if there was any history of this disease. The family was able to confirm a probable case with Lucia's brother. The operative word was probable, because although the symptoms and rapid progression of the disease were identical to Creutzfeldt Jakob, without a brain biopsy or autopsy, neither of which were performed on the brother, there can be no confirmed diagnosis.

Although there was some relief in finally having a strong sense of the nature of Lucia's illness, the prognosis was not good. Patients with the disease usually died within a year after the initial onset of symptoms. At the time there was no known treatment protocol to reverse the disease, halt it or even slow it down.

The battery of tests for Lucia also indicated a growth in one of her breasts. She was then automatically referred to an oncologist for an exam and further x-rays. I thought this referral was unnecessary under the circumstances, as did her daughters. As I previously mentioned, Lucia had been diagnosed with cancer years ago and had worked hard to bring it into remission. Though it was possible that the cancer had returned, certainly the course of her primary disease would take her life sooner than any tumor. It seemed paramount to keep Lucia as comfortable and safe as possible for whatever brief time she had left. The daughters cancelled the appointment with the oncologist and no further probing was done.

Meanwhile, the neurologist had contacted a colleague who had actually treated several people with Creutzfeldt Jakob and was familiar with the symptoms and its course. Lucia's neurologist strongly recommended that the daughters make an appointment with this physician as soon as possible. Caroline agreed to do this. Within two weeks Lucia was taken to the physician and the probability of Creutzfeldt Jakob was confirmed. At this point, I encouraged Caroline and Lena to request a referral for hospice services, which they did. Lucia was back in the nursing home, and within a day or two of her diagnosis, she developed another fever and was sleeping almost all the time. She stopped eating and was generally unresponsive. The hospice nurse explained to us that her bodily functions were rapidly shutting down and that death would be imminent, probably within the next day or so.

> Can you identify various ways Lucia's daughters advocated on her behalf?

The daughters and I alternately kept a vigil pretty much round-the-clock. Friends would come into Lucia's room and say their goodbyes. Later in the afternoon when Caroline came in, she took a swift inventory of the room and began to make several wonderful changes. After some initial tidying up, she checked with the nurse on duty to see if we could discontinue the supplemental oxygen. The machine is very noisy and did not seem to be a critical component in maintaining Lucia's comfort at this late stage. Caroline was clear that her mother would not want to die hooked up to any machines. With the nurse's permission, we turned off the machine and removed the tubing from her nose. Aah, the room already seemed much more peaceful. Caroline then asked permission to light a candle near her mother's bed in order to use a diffuser for essential oils. She put on some beautiful, devotional music. I couldn't get over the change in the room. Caroline's loving touches had lifted the energy tremendously, and the difference was palpable not only to us, but to the staff as well. The daughter created a sacred space—a loving cradle from which her mother could make her transition.

During part of the night, I lay down next to Lucia and tried to emulate her breathing, as a way of comforting her. When a woman is in active labor preparing to give birth, emulating her breathing pattern can help her remain calm and focused. I was taught that this same technique can be soothing and reassuring to someone who is dying. Periodically her eyes would flash open in what seemed like a panicked expression. Her breathing would become rapid and shallow. Caroline and I would encourage her to relax and let go—to follow the Light. Caroline assured her that she and Lena would be fine and she could leave whenever she felt ready. These episodes when she seemed to be so startled only lasted a few moments, but it seemed to us, each time they occurred, that that was going to be "it." It was a very long night for us all. Lucia was working so hard, her breathing was so labored that I had the sense that I was serving more as a midwife for a birth rather than a helper in death. Caroline, Lena and I tried to doze off in recliners that were made available for us, but sleep was beyond our grasp as we listened to Lucia's gurgling breathing, attending to any sudden changes in the pattern.

Sometime just prior to daybreak, Lucia's breathing started to slow down dramatically, with long pauses between each breath until finally there were no more. There was an immediate sense of quiet and calmness in the room. Lena had just left the nursing home less than a half an hour ago to prepare for work, so I went to the nurse's station to phone her. She arrived back within minutes. I kissed Lucia goodbye, hugged both daughters and left. This was the morning of March 10, several months since Lucia handed me her beautiful eggs and asked me to accompany her on this journey.

Of the many potent lessons for me in this situation, what stands out among them is that of communication. As Lucia's dementia increased at a dizzying pace, communication with her became a formidable challenge for all of us who cared for her. As I mentioned earlier on, although her words had the phonetic sounds of a Germanic language (she and her daughters spoke Dutch fluently), neither Caroline nor Lena could make any more sense out of her dialogue than the rest of us. But by observing her facial expressions and body language, it was clear that Lucia's communication was entirely meaningful for *her*.

> Do you feel comfortable communicating with patients suffering from advanced dementia? In addition to what was mentioned in the story, can you identify some other approaches that could facilitate meaningful exchanges in these situations?

I remember several occasions when Lucia was conversing with other patients at the nursing home. As they were also suffering from some degree of dementia, their conversations made absolutely no sense to the casual eavesdropper. They carried on with each other as if they knew exactly what each one was talking about. Rapport, empathy and humor characterized these exchanges. It was amazing for me to observe, and it provided the key for my own communication with Lucia. It didn't matter whether I could attach literal meanings to her gestures and nonsensical words. As long as I could try to emulate the intonations of her voice, the expressions in her eyes and other cues from her body language, I too could show her that I was listening and cared about what she was feeling. I think we were very successful with this mode of communicating and it helped me realize that conveying a sense of love, care and acceptance need not be limited to a set vocabulary. Speaking from the heart is not dependent on words to make itself felt and understood. I am deeply appreciative of Lucia for her guidance in this discovery.

In her book, *The Wheel of Life* (listed in appendix), Elisabeth Kubler-Ross illustrates this phenomenon as she relates a story from her childhood. Confined to her hospital bed during a serious illness, Elisabeth describes her relationship with the child sharing her room:

> She drifted in and out of consciousness, so we never actually spoke. But we were very comfortable with each other, relaxed and familiar. We stared into each other's eyes for immeasurable periods of time. It was our way of communicating. We had long, deep and meaningful conversations without ever making a single sound. It was a kind of simple transference of thoughts. All we had to do was open our young eyes to start the flow. Oh, my, there was so much to say (p. 29).

Though many parts of her brain were shutting down at an alarming pace, like Alzheimer's on fast-forward, her capacity to express her feelings through her eyes never left her. Even during her final hours, as I mentioned, her eyes would open in a startled stare beyond us. I have a picture of Lucia taken at her daughter's house just a few days before her passing. She is holding her granddaughter on her lap, and the camera has captured such a loving, joyful expression of "oma," the grandmother in Lucia. Is the essence of a person's selfhood housed in the brain or the heart? At least in Lucia's case, I can confidently conclude it was the latter.

The other fond memory I hold of Lucia during those final days was the last walk we took together, outside the nursing home. It was a fairly warm day in early March and I carefully wrapped my arm around

Lucia to bolster her precarious balance. As tentative as her balance was, her stride was strong and purposeful. She so loved being out and about in the crisp, spring air. We both took many deep breaths, drinking in the beauty of the day. To me, it felt like the culmination of our friendship, especially this last leg of the journey we were committed to walking together.

Keys for Compassionate Care for the Dying

Offer realistic commitments. Don't make promises you might not be able to keep. Although my intentions were sincere, I may not have been able to keep my promise to Lucia that I would stay with her no matter what happened. What if she had returned to her family in Holland or a crisis had arisen in my own life? In either case, I would not have been able to follow through on my commitment. A more realistic and appropriate assurance in such cases would be to say, "I will help and support you as best I can."

Do you hear what I hear? Be cautious about projecting your own meanings onto exchanges you have with the dying. When Lucia handed me her precious hand-crafted eggs, I personalized this interaction and attributed to it my own symbolism and meaning. I cannot assume that it held the same meaning for Lucia. Remember, perceptions are subjective and may not accurately reflect the other person's point of view.

Watch your reactions. Be mindful of how you convey your emotions to a patient. Expressing shock or dismay when seeing discomforting changes may cause pain and feelings of shame. You will help them most by holding your impressions on the inside and maintaining your composure and nurturing demeanor on the outside.

Set the mood. Creating a harmonious environment for the dying person is a simple and valuable gift to offer. Whether it is dimming the lights in the room, playing some of the person's favorite music, lighting candles or simply tidying up the area around the bed, all of these touches can make a significant difference in the comfort of the patient and those attending her.

Be a breathing coach. When a woman is in active labor preparing to give birth, emulating her breathing pattern can help her remain calm and focused. This same technique can soothe and reassure someone who is dying, conveying a sense of comfort and intimacy. Some breathing patterns, however, may be difficult to emulate, such as shallow and rapid respirations. Just do the best you can.

Listen and watch for nonverbal cues. Relying on words alone to communicate is limiting. When patients are too ill to speak, it may be difficult for them to express their needs accurately. We can ease this frustration by listening intuitively and paying close attention to a wide range of nonverbal cues and gestures. It doesn't matter whether we can attach literal meanings to gestures or even to nonsensical words. As long as we emulate the intonations of someone's voice, the expressions in the eyes and other cues from body language, we can show that we care about what he is feeling. Speaking from the heart is not dependent on words.

Keys for Self-Care

Address your distress. In attending to the dying, don't ignore your own needs and assume that nothing can be done to make your job easier. For example, when you are trying to sleep in a room with a loved one who has gurgling breathing that prevents you from resting, ask about safe medications that can help minimize the gurgling sound or request a mild sedative for yourself. Your loved one will get better care from you if you get good rest. Be honest about your needs; martyrdom is not a requirement for good caregivers.

Learn to recognize when death is near. Knowing what to expect will help you remain calm and focused when caring for someone in the active dying phase of their terminal illness. For instance, a common sign of approaching death is long pauses between the breaths, known as apneic breathing. Refer to Appendix A, "Relevant Terms," for a complete list of signs and symptoms of impending death.

6

UNRESOLVED FAMILY DYNAMICS

In late spring, I received a phone call from the hospice volunteer coordinator, asking if I could take on a new patient. She explained that Rudi had congestive heart failure and diabetes. He spent most of the day in his recliner and needed assistance with his walker to get to the bathroom. His wife, Paige, was his primary caregiver. She needed volunteer coverage Tuesday and Thursday mornings so she could attend her exercise class. I was glad to be called and looked forward to meeting Rudi.

My first visit happened to be on Rudi's birthday. Just a few blocks from my own home, I arrived on my bicycle and was greeted at the door by his wife, Paige. We had just enough time for a brief introduction, as she was on her way out the door. Rudi was resting in his recliner by a large picture window. My first impression was how wasted his body looked—more like someone with cancer. His face was pale and taut. His hands rested on his blanket like a skeleton. But when I reached out my hand to him (and my hands were a lot colder than his!) he gave me a warm greeting and expressed his appreciation for my coming. We had no trouble striking up a conversation and I soon discovered what a wonderful storyteller he was. Rudi offered me a sweeping and engaging version of his life from early boyhood in Wyoming to the present in Montana. The highlight of the saga for me was hearing about his first wife, Katie. It was a romance fit for a screenplay. They met at a hot springs healing resort. Katie's family brought her to the mineral baths to receive therapeutic treatments for her multiple sclerosis. By Rudi's account, it was a match that was meant to be. He was in his early twenties and he had never before felt comfortable around women. Rudi had not experienced the good fortune of meeting a gal that he really wanted to get to know—until Katie came along.

It wasn't long after their first encounter at the spa that Rudi proposed. He had just enlisted in the service during World War II and he wanted to get married before he was sent overseas. At first Katie was doubtful. Why would Rudi want to hitch up with a cripple? "Because I love you," was all he could say. That was good enough for her. Katie's parents agreed to continue caring for their daughter until Rudi's return from duty.

He was only away for two years when Rudi received his honorable discharge from the army. I can only imagine what a joyful reunion theirs must have been. Rudi and Katie moved to Montana, where he attended college under the GI bill.

He successfully completed his program in mechanical engineering and, immediately upon graduating, commenced his own teaching career in the same department. Meanwhile, their family was growing. Their third child was not yet a year old when Katie was diagnosed with cancer. The house they were having built for them was near completion—the same house I was now sitting in. Rudi had seen to it that the kitchen was handicap-friendly; all the cupboards and countertops could be easily reached from a wheel chair. But the cancer spread quickly and Katie didn't live to enjoy all the customized touches that Rudi had designed for their home. She left Rudi a widower with three children to bring up, all under the age of eight.

I was very moved when Rudi spoke about Katie and his abiding affection for her. I haven't often come across a gentleman in "real life" who seemed so gallant in his love for his wife. The fact that their brief life together ended so tragically, while still in its prime, made his story all the more poignant.

Enter a young widow named Paige, stage left. Paige had lost her husband to a sudden heart attack and was also left with three young children. Mutual friends were convinced the happy ending to this tragedy was obviously to bring Rudi and Paige together. They got together all right, and based on the circumstances of their situation, it seemed like a good fit at the time. So, Rudi and Paige got married. Unbeknownst to the friends who set them up, however, they did not live happily ever after.

As soon as they were married, Paige and her children moved into Rudi's home—the home he designed for Katie. Paige had a difficult time with this arrangement, especially working in a kitchen designed for someone in a wheelchair. Although she had asked Rudi many times over the years to remodel the house or move into a new one, he adamantly refused. This created a hotbed of resentment between them. On several occasions, Paige vented her frustrations about her husband. But since most of my time was spent alone with Rudi while Paige was out and about, I definitely received more information from his perspective than I did from hers. Most of what Rudi shared was in the context of his storytelling. He was reviewing his life up to the present with me, and in the process it seemed like he was trying to sort out his unfinished business with Paige. During one of my visits I asked Rudi if I could see a picture of Katie, but he told me that Paige had destroyed all of the pictures of her shortly after their marriage. I was startled and upset by this news; it significantly marred my opinion of his wife. Perhaps my judgments were unfair, since I didn't inquire after Paige's side of the story. But she never volunteered any information about Katie and I never asked.

Paige led an active life—water aerobics, exercise classes, Bible study meetings and outings with family and friends—and therefore requested much more volunteer support than the usual caregiver. On average, there were three to four volunteers assigned to Rudi. This really wasn't a problem for the volunteers since Rudi was such a pleasant and engaging man to spend time with.

At one point, Paige wanted to go on an overnight camping trip with her family. Instead of private care being hired to stay with Rudi in her absence, the entire 24 hours was covered by volunteers. The volunteers were permitted to give their home phone numbers to Paige, if they wished. Normally, giving out home phone numbers was strongly discouraged for privacy reasons. Since then, the hospice administration has once again tightened up on this policy. But Paige did have several of the volunteer's phone numbers and, in my case, she never abused this arrangement.

My visits with Rudi continued throughout that summer. One day I noticed that he seemed upset about something. When I asked what was troubling him, Rudi replied that he had heard some distressing news the previous day. Back in January, he had some surgery done and spent several weeks recuperating at the nursing home. During his sojourn there, Rudi became quite fond of one of the nurses who cared for him. At the time, she was in remission from cancer. Her courage, kindness and sense of humor left an indelible impression on Rudi, as he continued to struggle with his own life-long health issues. Yesterday, Rudi learned that his friend was very sick again—her cancer had returned. The person who relayed this news was doubtful that she would survive. Rudi began sobbing as he was telling the story, and my sense was that losing this friend to cancer might be bringing up the loss of his first wife, together with the tears that he was now allowing himself to shed. I asked him if there was anything he would like to do in response to this news. Rudi said that he would like to somehow contact this nurse and tell her how much she had meant to him. He wanted to offer the same love and support to her that she had so generously offered to him. I suggested that we could send her a card with a personal note to her. Rudi thought that was a fine idea, and I offered to pick up one before the next visit.

Rudi was happy with the card I selected, so the next stage was to compose a letter. Rudi dictated his thoughts to me and I helped him along here and there. Satisfied with our draft, Rudi wanted to type it into the computer, which we did next. Finally, he selected a passage from the Bible, one that he had read on many occasions for memorial services. (Rudi was a Mason and officiated at many memorial services for fellow Masons.) With the card posted in Rudi's mailbox, our project was now complete, and I think he felt relieved that he had taken the effort to express his grief and to extend his love. He never did hear back from the nurse. When he learned of her death a few weeks later, Rudi seemed confident that she was in a better place and had an end to her suffering.

Among the stressors that Paige was experiencing in caring for her husband was food. He had specific and limited food preferences that she had a hard time adapting to. Whereas Rudi would have been content with pancakes, hot cereal and some soft vegetables as his daily diet, she was concerned that there should be more variety in his menu. Determined to balance Rudi's nutritional needs, Paige consistently served foods he either no longer had a taste for or found difficult to swallow. Rudi had difficulty swallowing most food and would typically go into coughing fits minutes after finishing a meal. When Paige brought up the issue one day while her husband was napping, I asked her if she had broached the topic of nutrition with any of the nurses. When she said no, I explained that making sure Rudi had a balanced diet was not really necessary. Terminally ill patients often don't have much of an appetite to begin with. Their taste for foods has usually changed drastically and they don't have the same food requirements as a healthy person.

On top of all these factors, when you weigh in Rudi's difficulty swallowing and his coughing spells, it stands to reason that he would be selective about what he ate. But Paige saw his persnickety attitude as another form of rejection and overall lack of appreciation for her caregiving. So, I made two suggestions. I encouraged Paige to just give

Rudi what he asked for and not to worry about whether his food choices constituted a balanced diet. Secondly, I said I would speak to his nurse to see if we could get a dietitian to visit them. Perhaps the dietitian could come up with some menu choices that would be easy for Paige to put together and easy for Rudi to get down. In the meantime, one of the hospice volunteers was providing Rudi with his daily dose of pancakes. She would make a big batch on the weekends and freeze them. Monday mornings, she would deliver the goods to Rudi, who was as pleased as could be with the special attention and with the pancakes!

Throughout the summer, Rudi took several spills, experienced some instances of incontinence and was generally becoming weaker. When Paige returned from her camping trip, she came down with a cold, which Rudi inevitably caught. He had a long history of lung conditions, stemming from an early childhood bout with rheumatic fever, from which he almost died. Any cold symptoms typically settled in his lungs, as did this one. Rudi's appetite decreased noticeably and fierce coughing fits left him exhausted. Paige was running out of steam as well, exhausted from the emotional and physical demands of caregiving. Something had to give. Rudi had made his wishes known on many occasions to various hospice workers, family and friends: he did not want to leave his home, period. Paige, on the other hand, was no longer physically or psychologically able to tend to his needs, and she felt they could not afford to hire private in-home care to take up the slack. Such expense would quickly drain what little assets they had. It was becoming more apparent that Paige was moving in the direction of placing Rudi in an in-patient facility. Unfortunately, the community where they lived does not have a hospice residential facility, so the choices were either a nursing home or respite care facility. Neither

> Does the hospice team advocate for the patient or for the caregiver, when clearly their needs and wishes are diametrically opposed?

choice was appealing to Rudi and he reiterated that he would be happiest at home. It was time for the hospice social worker to intervene.

Though Rudi believed staying home would make him happy, it was clear to many observers that friction between the couple was building to precipitous levels. Here is a classic example of being caught between the proverbial rock and hard place. The social worker arranged for the owners of the respite facility to come and visit with Rudi and Paige, to explain their services and accommodations. The social worker apparently hoped that if Rudi could get a better sense of the facility and its many "home-like" features, he would be more amenable to moving. Not so. Unfortunately the decision was taken out of his hands entirely when he overheard Paige telling a relative on the phone that Rudi would be moved into the respite facility the following week. When and why it became irrelevant that Rudi have equal say in this decision, I never understood. The page was turned, a decision was made and all I could do was support Rudi as best I could through the transition. I promised Rudi I would be there with him on moving day and I was.

I will never forget the tears that he spilled as we were preparing to leave the house. A home health aide was also at the house that morning. When Rudi started to cry, she immediately tried to hush him, offering assurances that he would like his new home. Though her intentions were certainly sincere, I feel it was a mistake to discourage Rudi from expressing pain and sadness in leaving his home, knowing he'd never return. I took the handles of Rudi's wheel chair and maneuvered him out the door. It was a sad farewell to a home that held many mixed memories for him. We then guided his wheelchair onto the ramp and into the van that would carry Rudi to his new home.

> Did the hospice team sufficiently advocate for Rudi?

Rudi seemed to adjust fairly quickly to his new surroundings. The staff at the respite center, like the rest of us, had no trouble getting to know and love Rudi. A recliner by the picture window was designated as "Rudi's chair." From this vantage point, Rudi could observe much of the activity around the house, and during my visits I would often hear tales about some of the notable happenings. As a part of a friendly and caring environment, which could also monitor and meet his ever-increasing physical needs, Rudi was being well served. That he never really accepted being taken out of his home, and was regularly asking when he might return, made me feel remorse. I know where I would want to be at the close of my life, and I only hope that those who are caring for me will be able to honor and fulfill this desire.

Autumn passed into winter and I kept up my weekly visits with Rudi. On snowy days the views outside the large windows were spectacular. On many occasions, a fire was burning in the hearth and Rudi especially enjoyed that. Mostly we would just chat comfortably during our visits like two old friends. He often asked me about my family and what we were up to, and I always got the sense that these were not just polite inquiries but that Rudi really cared. Rudi enjoyed reading and had a favorite author who wrote novels about the "wild west." The library carried the entire series, so I tried to keep Rudi well stocked. Some days he complained about his shoulder or arm being sore, so I would give him a gentle massage as he sat in his chair. Rudi thoroughly enjoyed being massaged, making it a pleasure to care for him in this way.

Paige came up to see Rudi every day and brought him the paper. She enjoyed people and had no difficulty finding things to talk about with the staff and residents. Rudi, on the other hand, was more soft-spoken and reserved. He often just sat back and listened while Paige chatted away happily. The tension in their relationship reduced dramatically since Rudi's move. No longer saddled with the burdens of being a caregiver, Paige was free to pursue her daily activities and social engagements. She did comment that it was very lonely in the house without Rudi. From what I gathered, this had been the first time in her life that she had ever lived alone. Paige wasn't the only one who seemed to be reaping some benefit from the arrangement. Since being at the respite center, Rudi's health seemed to stabilize. He was enjoying the home-made meals and actually seemed to be putting on some weight. Rudi's face was less gaunt and his color looked good.

The hospice team began wondering if we needed to discharge him from hospice care, as his six-month evaluation was coming up. The social worker broached this possibility with both Rudi and Paige, which sent Paige into a panic. She had come to rely heavily on us for emotional support and even though Rudi was being well cared for by all accounts, Paige was not ready to sever her ties with hospice. We discussed Rudi's case at the interdisciplinary meeting and finally decided to keep him on hospice. Though most of his symptoms were being well managed, he did have signs of edema, with swelling in his lower legs. The ongoing edema and overall decline in his condition would still qualify him for hospice care, together with the primary diagnosis of congestive heart failure.

Two of Rudi's children came to visit over Thanksgiving and I was able to meet them. As they both lived on the East coast, this was their first time seeing their father in his new environment. Apparently, they were very pleased with the respite home and at how well Rudi seemed to be doing here. They each thanked me for all the good care their father was receiving through hospice, and in particular, through the volunteers whose friendship has meant so much to Rudi. Not knowing when or if they'd ever see their father again, it seemed their visit was especially poignant.

Around Christmas time Rudi's edema seemed to be worsening. The swelling from his abdomen went all the way down his legs and was becoming alarming. The medication that had previously helped keep it in check was not working. The day after Christmas, Rudi was admitted into the hospital. Draining the fluid with a syringe did nothing to keep more from accumulating the following day. His belly was extremely swollen, as were his lower arms, hands, fingers and legs. He was sleeping almost continually now. Rudi could still be roused when visitors came, but was not able to converse more than a few minutes before dozing off again. Since Paige did not want any life-prolonging treatment, such as dialysis, the social worker for hospice arranged to transfer him to a nearby nursing home.

Rudi was aware that he had been moved once again and was presently in the nursing home, but he showed little interest in his surroundings. Even though he was sleeping most of the time, he still had an appetite and allowed staff and volunteers to spoon-feed him soft meals. After a couple of days, he showed signs of increased agitation. Rudi was picking at his bedclothes, and his yelling could be heard down the hall. These behaviors were so uncharacteristic of him, it was startling. He seemed almost delirious in his ranting. After adjusting his medication, these episodes subsided and Rudi seemed calm and comfortable. During the afternoon of his last day, Paige and I were visiting in his room. All of a sudden he awoke startled, and mumbled something. I called Paige to come closer to him, so we were each standing on either side of his bed. I told Rudi that she was right here with him and then I encouraged her to speak to him. Paige told him she loved him and then started to cry. Rudi fell back into a deep sleep and Paige left to go to a friend's house for dinner. Before I left, I made sure the staff knew to call me at home if there were any changes with Rudi.

> What were some of the indicators that Rudi was actively dying?

That evening my husband and I decided to go to a movie. I had been spending a lot of time at the nursing home and needed a break. I left instructions with our babysitter to call me immediately if the nursing home happened to call. She knew I was a hospice volunteer and I explained that I had a patient who was actively dying. Confident that I had my bases covered, I left for the movies and thoroughly enjoyed the comic relief it provided. Afterward, I dropped my husband off at home and proceeded to the nursing home. The night nurse intercepted me in the hall and told me that Rudi had died and that the funeral home had already picked up the body. I was shocked. She said someone had called and left a message at my home. But then, why didn't I hear anything from my babysitter?

I immediately went home and she was still there. The babysitter explained that indeed the nursing home had called when Rudi died. She told the nurse that I had gone to the movies and asked if she thought I should still be called. Understandably the nurse said no, that Rudi was dead and there was nothing more I could do. I believe there was something more I could do—to sit quietly with Rudi's body, in prayer, until the undertakers arrived. My reaction was disappointment in my babysitter that she had not followed my instructions, but also a sense of acceptance that this is how Rudi must have wanted it—no one in his room—not Paige, myself or another volunteer. And I also imagine he just didn't want me walking out on a good movie!

My daughter and I paid our respects to Rudi at the funeral home. My daughter had accompanied me several times when Rudi was in the respite home and wanted to say goodbye to him too. She brought along her violin and played him the song she was learning. I know this made him happy.

I phoned Rudi's daughter the day after her father died and listened as she shared her grief and tears. I filled her in on Rudi's last days and she was grateful to hear more details, having received some amount of information from Paige. She was so glad she had visited her father over Thanksgiving and had the chance to spend time with him while he was still relatively well. I was glad for her too.

Rudi always used to call me "darlin'" and I know I'm not the only lady friend who was so honored. It is in his memory that I am determined to see a hospice house established in my community—a home for people to die in dignity, comfort and beauty when they are unable to remain in their own homes.

Keys for Compassionate Care for the Dying

Check out hospice care. Many people are under the misconception that hospice is just for individuals with terminal cancer. However, there is a wide range of terminal illnesses that are managed under hospice care. At a physician's referral, a patient is eligible if he or she is expected to live six months or less and is no longer actively seeking a cure.

Tie up loose ends. Help patients with unfinished tasks—anything from writing and sending thank you notes to preparing their own memorial service. Helping Rudi compose a note to his ailing nurse gave him a creative outlet to express his appreciation for her care, process his grief and bring closure to that relationship. Actively grieving this loss may have even helped him on some level come to terms with his own approaching death. We can never know the full impact our actions have on others.

Food for thought. Be flexible in adapting to the changing food preferences of those who are terminally ill. Bear in mind that they often don't have much of an appetite and they don't need to eat the same kind of balanced diet a healthy person does. Since they may feel overwhelmed when presented with what appears to them as a huge plate of food, try offering very small portions of food at any one meal. Facing this may be difficult for you, especially when you are desperately trying to keep them well for as long as possible. Be gentle on yourself. Their rejection of food you have lovingly prepared for them is not a rejection of you.

Are alternative therapies safe? Alternative healing approaches, such as relaxation and visualization techniques, have been quite successful in easing discomfort for the terminally ill. However, certain alternative therapies may not mix well with allopathic medicines or with the patient's condition. For example, specific herbal treatments may interact negatively with certain drugs, and massage therapy would not be appropriate for patients with blood clots. Be open to alternative therapies that help the patient, but consult with the patient's nurse or physician before initiating them.

Keys for Self-Care

Go with the flow. Sometimes death throws you a curve ball. As I left Rudi's room to take a break, I was certain I would be back to sit with him one last time. Returning to the nursing home later that evening, only to find him gone, was jarring. My best-laid plans had come undone and I needed to find closure with Rudi in other ways. Anyone caring for the dying needs to find meaningful ways to say goodbye to the people they have served, such as viewing the body or attending a memorial service. Hospices typically offer regular memorial services to honor patients they have served. Family members, staff and volunteers are all welcome to these services.

Keys for Hospice Volunteers

Practice detachment. It can be unsettling to hear detailed and highly personal information regarding the marital or family dynamics of a patient. We inevitably develop close friendships with patients, especially when we have visited them for months on end. As a result, we may unwittingly be drawn into a web of unresolved emotions, sometimes pent up inside the patient or caregiver for an entire lifetime. While it can be tempting to take sides in familial disputes, situations are not always black and white. Be objective and maintain healthy boundaries in cases like this. Confer with your supervisor if at any point you feel overwhelmed or confused by family interactions.

Confer with the team. Talk with your team before offering additional services, such as cooking special food or transporting patients to appointments. This will help you evaluate whether your offer is appropriate and it will help the team document this in the patient's plan of care.

Debrief after stressful transitions. In the course of caring for the dying, we may witness events that concern us. Rudi's transfer from his beloved home to the respite care center triggered intense emotions, not only in me but in many members of the hospice team. It was a polarizing situation, depending on whose perspective you were most sympathetic to—Rudi's or his wife's. The team can gain clarity and perspective by participating in debriefing sessions following such episodes.

7

UNPREDICTABLE TIMING

Lisa had recently been transferred from an assisted living community to a nursing home. She had colon cancer that had metastasized to her rectum, leaving her in considerable discomfort most of the time. Lisa was receiving morphine through a bolus that she could self-regulate. Even with the morphine and a special cushion for her buttocks, the tumor on her rectum made sitting for any length of time an excruciating ordeal for Lisa. So it was not uncommon for her to spend much of her days lying on her side in bed. The quality of her life had taken a nosedive since her transfer to the nursing home; the staff at the assisted living facility was no longer capable of handling her mounting symptoms. The hospice nurse thought that she might enjoy getting out once in awhile to do some shopping, have some lunch or just go for a ride. As I was getting the essentials on Lisa, the volunteer coordinator warned me that Lisa could be ornery. She was not the easiest person to please, and several of the hospice nurses had encountered some difficulties with her in the past. This information left me a little nervous, but I was eager for a new patient, as it had been many months since I had been assigned to someone.

When volunteers complete their training and interview process, they are often dismayed that an entire year may pass without receiving a patient assignment. This lapse between assignments can also hold true for veteran volunteers as well. Typically the volunteer pool is much greater than the patient need. There are several reasons for this imbalance. In many situations, caregivers rely on family members, friends or their church community for back-up support. In addition, it can be difficult for people to understand the volunteer concept, accepting help with no strings attached. Finally, some patients just do not want a stranger around them during such a vulnerable time.

On Tuesday morning I found Lisa's room at the end of the corridor, directly across from the dining room. Both she and her roommate were sleeping so I quietly took a chair and sat down beside her bed. I sat for a few moments to collect myself, to silently take in Lisa and then gently called out her name. She startled awake and, more with a grimace than a smile, her eyes greeted me for the first time. I introduced myself as a hospice volunteer and Lisa remembered that the nurse had told her that someone would be coming. She apologized for not having any energy to go out today and seemed concerned that it was a waste of my time to come.

> Was the intensity of Lisa's pain a barrier to human contact? Did Lisa feel isolated inside her pain? Could this sense of isolation have exacerbated the suffering and depression she endured?

I assured her that it was perfectly fine with me if we just stayed in her room for today and used our time to get to know one another a bit. Lisa was awfully uncomfortable and it was easy to see that this fact alone made her short tempered with people. Listening to her speak about the current situation, she sounded depressed and just plain miserable. After she talked for a little while, sharing a few of the pertinent details of her condition, Lisa seemed exhausted. I offered to rub her feet, hoping this would relax her a little bit and distract her from the pain. Lisa enjoyed having her feet massaged, but ultimately it was too uncomfortable for her to lie on her back so we didn't continue very long. My first visit with her may have lasted less than an hour and I think it was a mixed bag. I felt insecure in witnessing and working around her intense pain. I had never been with someone before who seemed to be so constantly uncomfortable. But I was encouraged that Lisa had let me massage her—this showed some trust on her part—and that I seemed to be somewhat successful in giving her comfort.

Though it was originally established that I would visit with Lisa once a week, I knew that if I was going to make any meaningful contact in this relationship, I would need to visit more frequently. So I chose an optimal schedule of Tuesday and Thursday mornings and ran this by the volunteer coordinator. These times were incorporated into Lisa's plan of care. When I arrived the following Thursday, the hospice nurse was just beginning her visit with Lisa and was not sure how long she would need to be with her. I decided to leave and just come back the following week. Sometimes visits among hospice team members will overlap and this can be an opportunity for exchanging pertinent patient information. Unless they attend the weekly IDT meetings, volunteers don't have much contact with the nurses. So when a volunteer does happen to meet up with a nurse while visiting a patient, it can help the volunteer feel more integrated with the team.

During those months of visiting Lisa, I can vividly recall walking up the stairwell to her room, fairly nervous about what each visit would bring. Lisa was as unpredictable as Montana's weather, and the uncertainty of what to expect kept me in a perpetually humble and vulnerable state of mind. In spite of my insecurities around Lisa, or maybe because of them, our friendship seemed to blossom. I remember another attempt at massaging Lisa, this time her bare back as she sat tentatively on the edge of her bed. I had ridden my bicycle to the nursing home on this early spring day and even though I tried rubbing my hands vigorously to warm them up, Lisa just about jumped out of her skin when my hands touched her back. She yelled out to "rub hard, damn it," and get some heat going. I kept at it for a little while but then she told me to stop—again it was

> What value to the volunteer can you see in Lisa's unpredictable nature?

too uncomfortable for her to sit up. I felt useless. I apologized to Lisa, knowing I messed up and had unintentionally caused her even more discomfort with the jolt of cold from my hands on her bare skin. She in turn told me a story about her own cold hands.

When Lisa was a young woman, she lived with her widowed mother in Montana and helped take care of her younger siblings. One cold, winter evening the neighbors came over for a visit—a young man and his mother. They stayed for an hour or so and when it was time to leave, Lisa offered to go outside with the young man while he cranked up the motor. (Automobiles in those days were started, not by an ignition, but by the turn of a good, strong arm.) Lisa thought her muscles were as good as any and offered to do the job herself. When the motor turned over, she was pleased but not surprised. As the young man went to thank her by shaking the hand on that impressive arm, he was startled by how cold her hand was. He said to Lisa, "Young lady, you have mighty cold hands there, but for sure a warm heart." And with those words of endearment, their courtship officially began. So, as Lisa lay on her side recounting that story, she ended with the same message for me. "Young lady, you have mighty cold hands there, but for sure a warm heart." And with her words and that twinkle in her eye, I felt redeemed. I knew we had crossed a barrier and that our friendship had just begun.

Shortly into my visits with Lisa, she had a breakthrough in her pain management. Her oncologist injected the area around her tumor with a long-lasting numbing agent. This, combined with an adjustment in her morphine dosage seemed to significantly alleviate Lisa's pain. Her energy and spirits started to improve noticeably. Every morning after getting herself bathed and dressed, she'd help out in the dining room, getting the tables set for breakfast. Also part of her morning routine was updating the date and weatherboard in the hallway. Lisa was engaging in life again and it was so heartening for all of us to see. She and I would often go for a drive during our visits. On one occasion she wanted to go to K-Mart to look for some short-sleeve summer blouses.

Lisa made it clear that she did not particularly enjoy shopping, nor was she very good at it. I told her not to worry. I was a great shopper and felt confident I could help her find exactly what she was looking for.

I soon realized that part of the reason Lisa had such a hard time shopping was that she had numerous requirements for the particular item she was looking for. With her shirts, for example, she needed short sleeves, a pocket in the front, a pretty print or floral design to her liking *and* they had to cost nearly nothing. It took some doing, but I was able to find two shirts that met all of these criteria. And in spite of herself, I think she was pleased. I asked her if she ever considered shopping at thrift stores, since I knew she had difficulty spending very much money on clothes. Lisa was amenable to my suggestion so we made a quick stop at one of the local thrift stores. She and I had a great time finding all sorts of clothes that fit her style. However, Lisa was getting nervous because she had only brought so much money with her, and we were going way over her budget. I offered to loan her the extra money until she got her next monthly check, but she would have none of that. The mere thought of being in debt made her skin prickle. So, Lisa selected two items out of the pile we had gathered, paid for her clothes, and left with more self-discipline than I could have mustered in her shoes!

One day I arrived to find Lisa all ready to go out for a walk. It was a warm summer's day, so I suggested that she put on her sunbonnet and glasses. I had picked out a green gingham hat for Lisa during one of my visits to the thrift store and it suited her to a tee! She was just my height, not quite five feet, and this made us perfect walking buddies. Arm in arm, we strolled out of the nursing home to our destination—a small park by a creek several blocks away. On the way, Lisa stopped and examined various trees, shrubs and flowers, telling me their names and perhaps some other incidental information about them. She was soaking it all in, the smells and the textures, and her memories cascaded around us as we walked.

Reaching the park, Lisa was worn out so we sat for a spell at one of the picnic tables. She told me about floating down this very creek as a child and what fun she and her friends had had that day. She told me about her first experience with childbirth—watching her nephew being born. Lisa was still a child when her elder sister was ready to give birth. The sister was at a small birthing hospital and Lisa wanted to watch, so she came along. According to Lisa, the nurses didn't think she belonged there and told her to go home to her mama. But Lisa thought differently, so she stayed. The next day at school Lisa couldn't wait to tell her classmates where babies *really* come from. Lisa giggled as she remembered telling the children that her nephew came out of her sister's "cunt." I can only imagine the look on that poor teacher's face as Lisa proudly relayed her information to the class. Lisa was just as plucky now as she was as a child and I loved her for it.

Like the telling of that story, we shared several good belly laughs during our visits together. One day we were in Lisa's room and she wanted to change her blouse. After I helped her with the sleeves, I started buttoning the tiny buttons for her. Don't you know it took me *three* tries to get those buttons lined up properly! We laughed and started cracking jokes about how many friends it takes to button a shirt!

After a couple of shopping excursions, we did what girls do—we treated each other to lunch. At a little café close to the nursing home, Lisa and I ordered hamburgers, French fries and root beer sodas. She didn't know how long it had been since she had had a root beer, and I could tell she was savoring it. Though typically Lisa did not have much of an appetite these days, she polished off most of her meal. As we ate, Lisa paid close attention to our neighboring patrons. She was curious and observant for no apparent reason, other than it was life unfolding around her and she wanted to gobble it up!

On occasion Lisa received letters from her friends but found it difficult to gather her thoughts to reply. When hearing about her frustration, I offered to help her draft some letters. Lisa would dictate and occasionally I would prompt her along with a suggestion or two. We wrote two letters like this and I think it was a great relief to Lisa to be able to respond to her friends.

There were days when Lisa was too weak or in too much pain to leave her bed, and during one such visit I noticed a religious magazine on her bedside table. I asked her if she would like me to read from the magazine and she said fine. It was a daily meditation on different passages from the Bible. I found the day's meditation and began reading. Lisa followed me closely with her eyes and when I was done she complimented me on my reading. She said that like many other activities these days, she found it nearly impossible to concentrate on what she was reading and therefore had great difficulty making sense out of it all. But when I read it to her, she was better able to follow along. This began another ritual of ours, my reading to her from her prayer magazine.

Another relief for Lisa was finishing her hand-crocheted tablecloth that she intended to give to her granddaughter. This project was many months in the making, and all that was left to be done was finishing up the border. Lisa did not have the stamina to accomplish this, so her daughter stepped in to complete the task. When the daughter returned it, Lisa showed it to me before passing it on to her granddaughter. She was so proud and delighted to have finally accomplished her task that it was as if a burden was being lifted from her.

Lisa had developed a comfortable and loose set of beliefs about God, Jesus and an afterlife over the years. Some of her family members had a difficult time accepting Lisa's right to hold her own beliefs and continually pressured her to conform to their particular faith tradition. During one of our conversations, Lisa shared with me a childhood memory of being shamed by another little girl as she came out of a Sunday service one morning. Lisa, never having attended this particular church before, was spotted in the congregation by this child, a schoolmate of Lisa's. As Lisa was exiting the church, this girl approached and made some disparaging remark that Lisa's soul was so foul (for not being a regular churchgoer) that she shouldn't have even been allowed inside.

Thankfully, one of the teachers at their school was standing close by and overheard this remark. She swiftly reprimanded the child for her brazenness and sent her away. Privately, the teacher assured Lisa that she was as worthy as anyone else in that church and that God loved her as much as anyone. The teacher's support was a balm for Lisa; she told me that she went to this woman on other occasions as well, when her spirit needed some bolstering. When Lisa would occasionally express self-disparaging remarks or doubt her worthiness before God, I would remind her of this teacher and ask her what she thought this woman would say to her now, if she were sitting beside Lisa's bed instead of me. Although she never expressed a fear of dying, Lisa did battle with uncertainty about exactly what would happen after her death and about how God would ultimately receive her. The spiritual care coordinator for hospice was visiting her periodically, so I hope Lisa was able to find some solace in their conversations.

Our last outing together was visiting the old homestead of her brother-in-law. Lisa was not sure if the house was still standing or not—both her brother-in-law and wife were long deceased. But she wanted to go check it out, so off we went. Lisa was a good navigator and was able to get us to the area from sheer memory, without mishap. Sure enough, the house was still there, though quite dilapidated. There was also an old car parked alongside the house and we wondered out loud if anyone could possibly be living in that heap of rotting wood and shingles. Lisa did not want to find out, so we turned the car around and started for home.

In mid-August I was preparing to leave with my family on vacation. We would be gone for almost two weeks and I knew that the chances of Lisa being alive when I got back were 50-50 at best. I have no doubt that this fact probably crossed Lisa's mind as well. But she encouraged me with enthusiasm, telling me to have a great time. I told her I would miss her, and would send her a post card. Lisa said she'd be happy to receive it. With those parting words, we gave each other a squeeze and said goodbye.

> Is it hard for you to leave on a trip, knowing your patient, friend or family member might not be alive when you return? Is it difficult to say goodbye under these circumstances?

I phoned the nursing home almost immediately upon my return, and although she was still with us, the news was not very good. The nurse on duty informed me that Lisa was sleeping all the time now and had stopped eating and drinking the day before. Later that day, when I arrived at the nursing home, Lisa was curled up in bed and could not be aroused. I was saddened by her sudden and sharp decline. As a volunteer, you know that the people you visit are on the verge of death, but with Lisa that was not at all the focus of our time together. She wanted to squeeze out every last bit of life left on her plate and that's what our companionship was all about—the squeezing, the smelling, the seeing, the touching, the tasting—and best of all, the laughing. We celebrated her living—to the very end.

Then my bedside vigil with Lisa began. I started coming to see her twice a day, working it into my daily schedule. At this point her relatives were notified by hospice that she could die anytime now. The hospice nurses encouraged the family members to come and for someone to stay overnight with Lisa because they were concerned about her falling out of bed. Apparently she had fallen recently during the night while trying to get out of bed. A group of rather frazzled family members soon arrived from all parts of the map. As with the children's game "Telephone," it is almost predictable that the original message will be significantly altered during its repetition around the circle.

Such was the case with Lisa's family. Though it was never stated by the hospice nurses exactly when Lisa would die (members of any hospice team typically know better than to predict the time of death; we've all been wrong too many times!) the message that got passed around the family was: she could go any minute now and you had better hustle if you want to get there before she does. This misinformation placed an enormous amount of stress on an already strained family. The stress soon turned into resentment directed toward Lisa and even toward hospice. Apparently, during the course of Lisa's long bout with cancer, she had been close to death before. In that particular instance, the doctors never expected her to recover from a surgery that turned out to be much more invasive and difficult than was expected. The family was called to her bedside. But recover she did, and some family members were now feeling that they had been called out on a wild goose chase once again. Although it was clear to hospice and the nursing home staff that Lisa was dying, and any chance of her bouncing back again was out of the question, there was still no way of predicting just how long her dying process would take.

Not all her relatives were feeling "put out" by these uncontrollable circumstances. Lisa's granddaughter, Jessie, was content to sit by her grandma's side and wait. She was an attractive woman, almost child-like in appearance, with freckles speckled all over her face and a long auburn braid running down her back. With her calm and gentle manner coupled with her deep affection for her grandma, Jessie and I hit it off right away. Jessie was given a five-day leave from her job and stayed right beside Lisa for most of that time. Although she was sleeping and unresponsive for the most part, occasionally Lisa would startle awake and try to raise herself up to sitting. During these episodes, she seemed agitated and disorientated. In these moments when Lisa was awake, she sometimes would say, "Don't let me fall; don't let me fall!" Other times, it was only possible to catch a word or two of what she was saying. If I was present during

> Should these types of utterances be taken literally? What could this mean on a symbolic level?

these semi-lucid intervals, I would tell Lisa who was in the room with her and encourage the family to speak with her.

Aside from Jessie and one daughter-in-law, the other relatives were not very communicative with Lisa. The days were dragging on and there was not much change in Lisa's condition from one day to the next. She hadn't eaten or taken any fluids for over a week now. At one point her breathing became full of mucus and noisy, which is sometimes called "the death rattle." Her toes were a little bluish, but we couldn't be sure if that was from bruising when she had fallen out of bed or a decrease in circulation. Her vital signs were still stable, but her breathing did not sound good. I thought there was a pretty good chance that Lisa would die during the night. However, when I returned in the morning, her breathing sounded normal again and the nurse said there wasn't much happening. None of us could figure out what Lisa could be hanging on for. Everybody that was going to come had arrived and some had turned around and left again. We all brainstormed together, yet nobody had any ideas as to why Lisa seemed to be literally "hanging on for dear life." There was no question that she had a strong heart, which seemed to be compensating for her other failing organs. Lisa's tenacity for life, even on the threshold of death, was proving as fierce as her demeanor.

Jessie's leave was up and she needed to drive back home. It was hard for her to say goodbye to her grandma, but I assured her that I would continue keeping the vigil. Two days after Jessie's departure, Lisa was running a temperature and her blood pressure started dropping. By now her body had developed bedsores, despite all our efforts to keep her well positioned and turned frequently; she also had sores in her mouth, her face had sunken in and she was not much more than bare bones. I sat with her a little while that morning, but did not feel her extremities chilling down or turning bluish. Sometimes we'll see a breathing pattern where there are rapid respirations followed by long periods (5–30 seconds) of not breathing. These are called Cheyne—

Stokes respirations, and Lisa had been having these episodes for several days.

When I left I had no idea if Lisa's dying process would linger on much longer or not. Her daughter-in-law was going to stay for most of the day, and I was glad that Lisa would not be alone. All that day, I received no phone call, so I planned to return to the nursing home after dinner. I arrived shortly before 7 pm and was met at the nurse's station by the social worker. Lisa died at 6 pm, just as the residents were filing into the dining room for dinner, directly across the hall from her room! Her daughter-in-law had gone home for dinner, less than an hour before. If you've ever spent any time visiting in a nursing home, you'd know that meal times are the most hectic times of day. Lisa picked her time for her own reasons, and as with many other aspects of her living and dying, they will remain an enigma to those who loved her, but could never quite figure her out.

At Lisa's funeral I was disturbed by the insensitivity of the minister's comments. I've never before or since attended a memorial service where the deceased was actually maligned—by the minister, no less! He made it very clear that Lisa's salvation was not at all certain, based on her poor relations with her family and Lisa's apparent reticence in turning her life over to Jesus. I don't know why he chose to bring family tensions and personal spiritual matters into his sermon. His remarks came across to me as some kind of threat that we may end up with the same sorry fate as Lisa if we're not careful. If I hadn't been representing the hospice team at that service, I would have questioned the minister afterwards. As it was, I went up to Jessie and hugged her tight. I told her that I felt the minister's remarks were out of line—that her grandmother was a fine person and she should remember her that way. She nodded through her tears. We held each other for a moment and then I left.

Sometimes it is hard to listen to religious moralizing during what is meant to be a celebration of a person's life. The same holds true when a minister admonishes family and friends not to grieve because their loved one is in a better place. But the way this minister vilified Lisa's character, in order to emotionally manipulate his audience, was cheap and unconscionable in my opinion, an unwarranted ending for a remarkable woman.

Keys for Creating Compassionate Care for the Dying

Tune in. Being perceptive goes beyond active listening skills. Noticing the personal objects around the patient's room, such as photographs, books or crafts, will help you get to know her better and enable you to find meaningful ways to interact.

Care for the whole person. The dying have needs beyond the scope of their disease. Assisting them to complete meaningful tasks can give them immense satisfaction and a sense of peace. Depending on the help you provide, you may even be able to help them finish something that they can give a loved one as a precious legacy.

Follow your heart. There is no limit to the comfort you can offer patients in their final days when drawing from the wellspring of your own intuition and compassion. In Lisa's case, to console her in the present I reminded her of a significant person from her past whose memory had bolstered her throughout her life.

Don't hesitate to say goodbye. Any visit may be your last, so never hesitate to say goodbye to someone if you are uncertain whether he or she will still be alive for your next scheduled visit. An excellent resource on this topic is Ira Byock's book *The Four Things That Matter Most: A Book About Living* (listed in Appendix B, "Selected Readings"). Using his four simple statements: *please forgive me, I forgive you, thank you* and *I love you* can be instrumental in bringing healing and closure, not only at the bedside of the dying but throughout our lives.

Accept that death has its own timetable. Some people linger on in their dying process even when we think they are on the verge of passing on. Although this can be hard on a family, especially for those who have traveled some distance and are anxious to return home, it is not unusual. To cope with the variable nature of the dying process, be aware of the signs of active dying (included in appendix A, "Relevant Terms") and understand that the timing of this final passage is not something anyone can predict. It may be best to say goodbye to a loved one and communicate any final sentiments so you can be free of regret in case you are not present during their last moments.

Take advantage of interfaith care. In hospice, spirituality is not based on any one dogma or religious denomination. Spiritual care coordinators are sensitive and respectful of the patient's own beliefs and spiritual orientation. Their role is to support the patient within the context of the individual's own belief system. Often the spiritual care coordinator may simply act as an adjunct to the patient's own minister, rabbi or priest.

Keys for Hospice Volunteers

Get involved. In addition to visiting patients, there are many ways to support hospice with a variety of skills. Public speaking, fundraising, coordinating special events, helping in the office or maintaining the hospice library are all viable ways to become involved.

Check first. If you need to change your assigned visiting schedule with a patient, confer first with the volunteer coordinator. This will help to avoid overlapping visits from various team members. Any changes in hospice services also need to be documented in the patient's plan of care.

Be understanding of scheduling conflicts. There are handy scheduling tools available to minimize overlapping visits, such as large dry-erase boards posted in the hospice office. Each patient is listed as well as the daily schedule of visits from various team members. The board provides a quick overview of the nature and frequency of hospice services currently being offered each patient. Nurses and other team members may occasionally need to see a patient during your scheduled time. In this instance, you could be asked to cut short your visit.

Getting to know you. Integration between volunteers and staff varies from agency to agency. Create and take advantage of all opportunities for the two groups to interact, whether through social gatherings or educational seminars.

Cause no harm. The notion of developing a friendship with a patient sends up red flags for some hospice supervisors. They are necessarily cautious about maintaining boundaries and protecting patients. Friendships have not surfaced with all my patients, but when they have, it was a fortunate experience on both ends. A good rule of thumb for forming "friendships" is that the patient's needs come first. If I find that any aspect of my relationship or self-disclosure with a patient is serving more my own needs than the needs of the patient, this is a clear sign that there might be problems.

8

EASING A MOTHER'S PAIN

Several years ago I received a call from my father in New York City. He told me he had run into one of my childhood friends in our neighborhood. Dad went on to explain that Debbie was living back home with her parents and taking care of her mother, Betty, who had lung cancer. He offered me their phone number and I gave Debbie a call. It was wonderful to hear her voice again, especially her laughter. We had lost touch during high school, nearly thirty years ago. I explained to her that I worked with hospice as a volunteer and asked if she could share some of the details of Betty's illness. Apparently her daughters, Debbie and Dawn, started noticing that something wasn't right in the spring of 1998. They observed that Betty was having difficulty conversing with them. She struggled to find words and seemed increasingly unable to express herself and her feelings accurately. Betty also exhibited confusion about everyday activities, such as using shampoo instead of soap to wash her body. Normally a very active woman, having raised a family of five children, Betty became unusually tired and listless. She had to take naps just to get through the day. The situation that seemed to startle Betty the most was finding herself in the bank to cash a check one day and being unable to sign her name. Finally her daughters urged her to have a consultation with a neurologist; they feared she was exhibiting early signs of Alzheimer's. Not long afterwards a diagnosis of lung cancer, with metastases to the brain and bone, was confirmed instead.

Betty's grown children decided that Debbie would become Betty's primary caregiver and that two of her four siblings would pay her a certain amount each month for this service. So Debbie and her teenage son, Michael, moved out of their apartment and moved in with Betty and her husband, Ray. When Betty's cancer was diagnosed, it had already metastasized. Brain surgery was scheduled a week later. A ten-day round of full brain radiation followed the surgery. Though Betty pulled through this ordeal, neither the surgeon nor the oncologist was optimistic. They predicted she would have six months to a year of life, at best.

Betty's short-term memory was all but obliterated by the combination of the tumor, surgery and radiation. Although she was told about her cancer and prognosis at this time, she had no recollection of it later on. During my phone conversations with Betty, she often mentioned that she had never been told about the cancer and this seemed to bother Betty a great deal. Another difficult side effect of her treatments was her hair loss. When her hair finally grew back, it was sparse and coarse, totally unlike her original hair. Betty also developed sensitive bumps on her scalp and high forehead, which could be very painful at times. Debbie had to take great care when bathing her mother's head.

Although her eldest daughter brought her a wig, Betty hardly ever wore it, preferring a simple turban around her head, or nothing at all. But it always seemed to disturb Betty to see herself in the mirror or to run her fingers across those bumps.

In April of 1999, almost a year after Betty's initial diagnosis, she underwent lung surgery followed by radiation treatments for a growing tumor. Debbie remembers this episode as being remarkably uneventful compared to the brain surgery. Betty healed quickly from the surgery and had no major side effects from the radiation on her chest. The only thing noticeable after the treatments was that Betty's skin was very dry around the area that had received the radiation. Debbie said it felt like sandpaper, and although she regularly applied a strong skin moisturizer to the area, it never returned to normal.

Right around the time I initially contacted Debbie, which was March 2000, a clinical trial was about to commence with a new cancer drug. Betty's physician encouraged her to participate, and this meant a round of tests to determine whether she was a suitable candidate for the drug. Weeks of anxious waiting went by before Betty received confirmation in May that she could participate in the clinical trial. Betty always seemed to me a little ambivalent about doing the trial, but her family had renewed hope. First of all, it meant that Betty had to make frequent visits to her doctor's office and sometimes to the hospital for tests and checkups. These trips were always an ordeal for her and she dreaded them. Another source of anxiety was taking the pills. Although Debbie was responsible for administering all of Betty's medications, Betty would often ask whether it was time to take her pills yet. She felt very anxious about this.

Prior to starting the trial drug, Betty's pain was swiftly beginning to escalate. Debbie was concerned that she would have to resort to morphine because the milder analgesics were not adequately addressing her mother's pain (see note on the misconceptions about opioids for treating pain at the end of this chapter).

Betty was well into the trial (about a month), her pain symptoms decreased dramatically, to the point that she wasn't taking any medication for pain, aside from an occasional Tylenol. In addition to significantly extending Betty's life (she lived three years, one week and four days beyond her diagnosis date), the greatest benefit of the clinical trial drug was its effectiveness in her pain management.

Betty remembered me from my childhood days and was happy that Debbie and I had reconnected. I asked Betty if I could call her once a week—this was before I had heard about *Tuesdays With Morrie*—and she thought this would be fine. So we set our phone conversations for Wednesday mornings. Betty and I arranged it so that my calls would come after her morning television programs, which were an important part to her day.

My recollections of these phone calls, which went on for about a year, are many. We usually talked for about 20 minutes or so. Whenever Betty got tired or ran out of things to say, she would pass the phone to Debbie. We missed some weeks when Betty had a doctor appointment or wasn't feeling well or if I was on vacation. But mostly we remained faithful to each other and to our weekly connection. Betty was always candid with me about how the cancer was impacting her life, especially with regard to her relationship with her family. Since all our contact (with the exception of my visit to NYC) took place over the phone, I could not rely on other clues, such as body language or environment, to help me get reacquainted with Betty. My skills in reflective listening were certainly useful during these calls.

For years Betty's fortitude and nurturing held her family together. As a young child I always remember feeling welcome in her home. I have memories of Betty sitting at the kitchen table, looking out the window. When I would come to the door she greeted me with a warm smile and weary eyes. Her eyes seemed to be sad as well because she did not have an easy life. Betty was a homemaker in every sense of the word and took great care of all her children, under challenging financial and marital circumstances. My most vivid childhood memory of Betty was when I was over at the house one day I told her that I knew how to dance ballet. Her eyes lit up and she asked me if I would dance for her. In fact, I only imagined myself as a dancer, having had no formal lessons. I danced dramatically for her, but certainly without any recognizable skill. I could see that Betty had realized she had been duped, but tactfully praised me for my performance.

On the phone with me she shared that she didn't have the strength to care for her family anymore. Betty began distancing herself from them emotionally, and this caused her great angst at times. In the past, she always shopped for birthday and Christmas presents for her five children and five grandchildren. Betty took great delight in finding out just what they wanted and doing her best to please them. But her cancer left her too emotionally drained and physically exhausted for these activities. Occasionally, Debbie would take her mother to a shop in the neighborhood to pick out a gift or a card for someone, but as the illness wore on, these excursions tapered off. Soon Betty was reluctant to go outside at all. It was if the world was moving too fast for her and the pace was altogether exhausting. She told me she felt like an outcast because of her cancer. Nobody could understand what she was going through, she said, and if strangers sometimes glanced at her, she would feel self-conscious and ashamed of the cancer.

Like most women of her generation, Betty's role in the family was that of a caregiver. She loved her children and grandchildren unconditionally, and was available to them in good times and bad. But the cancer stripped her of that aspect of her identity, and Betty suffered considerably as a result. Some of her children were unable to accept the reality of her illness and the subsequent inability to emotionally take care of them anymore. They persistently tried to pull Betty back into their own worlds, interests and needs, while more and more, Betty refused to go. This created tension and pain for everyone, but I think especially for Betty.

An example of this situation played out in taking car trips. Living in New York City, it was always a treat to escape for a day, to visit family, go shopping or just take a ride out in the country. Often one of Betty's children would pick her and Debbie up and take them for a drive. The time came when these trips were no longer a pleasant diversion for Betty, but an exhausting ordeal. Sitting in the car for long stretches was painful, but the children could not see this. Aside from Debbie, who could read her mother inside and out, it was difficult for the rest of them to realize and accept that their efforts to relate to Betty were drastically missing the mark.

For Christmas that year, one of Betty's daughters wanted to bring her family, which consisted of her husband and two young boys, four and six, over from England. Under normal circumstances Betty would have welcomed such a visit and spent many days happily occupied with preparations. But things hadn't been normal for Betty in a long time, and she felt extremely anxious about this visit. Betty lived in a small apartment and worried that having to accommodate four extra people would put her over the edge. Her nerves were so raw that typically any excessive noise or commotion was quite unsettling for her. Betty fretted about this visit for weeks, not knowing how she was going to cope. The plane tickets had already been purchased so there wasn't any easy way out. The siblings either couldn't or wouldn't accommodate them, and financial restraints did not allow for any other choices.

The daughter's need was for her and her family to spend one last Christmas with Betty. Certainly, on the face of things, this is a legitimate desire. But Betty's need was for a peaceful and low-key environment. This is another example of the conflicting needs of the patient and the family. Unfortunately, at least from my perspective, the family's needs often win out in these types of scenarios. I say unfortunately, because the family is usually so focused on their own imminent sense of loss and grief that it can overshadow the needs of the one who is dying. In such cases, especially with the elderly, they simply do not have the strength, either physical or emotional, to fight their own battles beyond the struggle to get from one day to the next. In this case, Debbie, as the primary caregiver, was aware of the extraordinary stress that this visit would bring to bear not only on Betty, but on herself as well. Debbie felt her younger sister's needs and expectations of their mother were entirely inappropriate and out of sync with her current condition. However, Debbie and Betty felt that it would be easier in the long run to allow the visit to proceed rather than to deal with the aftermath of hurt feelings and recriminations, if they were told not to come. So the English contingency arrived and there were high points and low points throughout their stay. They did end up spending two days out of the week with friends in Connecticut, which helped significantly. All in all the visit went well, although I'm sure everyone was greatly relieved when it was over.

After Betty's various radiation treatments, her appetite was significantly diminished, as well as her taste for food. She subsisted on the bare minimum of nourishment and her wasting body showed it. Her foods of choice were oatmeal, dry toast, tomatoes and cheese, chicken and mashed or baked potatoes smothered in butter. But Betty's special treat was her Yankee Doodles. I think watching her favorite TV shows and enjoying a Yankee Doodle and milk were what she looked forward to most in her day—next to her naps. Napping gave Betty an opportunity for peace and quiet, something that eluded her during most of her day. Throughout her illness, her nerves suffered greatly and she would become easily distraught over any kind of problem that arose in the household. Betty couldn't tolerate noise or bickering and she seemed especially intolerant of her husband. If she quietly swallowed grievances about her husband over the course of her marriage, Betty was definitely not going to swallow them anymore! She just didn't have the energy or desire to be anything other than totally authentic in her feelings and communications.

This is often the case with people who are dying—they are stripped to the bare bones. There is no more pretense and, when you look into their eyes, it's a straight shot to their soul. This is one of the main reasons I enjoy this work so much. I think her husband handled these changes in Betty mostly by drifting into the background or by leaving the house for long stretches of time. He certainly took no initiative in her care or comfort; maybe this was partly due to Betty's overt rejection of him. Whatever the reasons, his involvement with the family at this time boiled down to being present for meals, staying home with Betty for short stints when Debbie had to go out and driving Betty to her doctor appointments. Particularly taxing on her were these trips to the doctor or hospital. Betty had questions she wanted to ask her doctor—like, why did she have so much trouble walking or why was she so tired all the time. These were symptoms that were obviously related to her illness, but because of Betty's mental impairments, she had great difficulty understanding and remembering this. When I would ask her about these visits with her doctor, she always seemed to feel let down. Unfortunately for Betty, the doctor was not able to offer the support and human connection that she needed from him.

On nice days, Debbie would take her mother in the wheelchair to a nearby park. Here they would sit companionably and feed the pigeons. During the course of Betty's illness, I was able to visit her one summer and, with peanuts in hand, we headed to the park to feed the pigeons. But I remember that she did not want to feed the pigeons that day, although she looked on as my four-year old daughter swiftly dispersed the entire bag of nuts to our congregation of birds. Later on at the playground, I noticed Betty was looking despondent and asked what the matter was. She had spent many afternoons here with her children and grandchildren, but she said that she didn't belong here anymore. It was for the young—not for her.

> How would you interpret Betty's feelings about visiting the playground? Do they indicate a sense of closure or isolation and withdrawal from life…or both?

I will always be grateful for this opportunity to have spent some time with Betty in person. It felt very easy to be in her company and I got a deeper sense of how she was coping with her illness. I learned what aspects of her environment gave her comfort and peace and what contributed to her sense of anxiety, depression and exhaustion. I relished her authenticity, experiencing her essence. This was a tremendous gift Betty extended to me; it is fortunate for me that I was awake enough to be able to receive it.

Volunteers who spend time with individuals in the later stages of terminal illness can reap many gifts depending on how fully present they are during each visit, how empty they are of any expectations or agenda, how capable they are of accepting the individual unconditionally and how comfortable they are simply sitting in the silence. So much can be communicated without words, and in fact, quite often a patient is too tired or too weak to talk. Just the presence of a caring companion at the bedside can convey enough serenity to bring comfort and ease some of the fear and loneliness of dying.

When Betty stopped wanting to go to the park, Debbie would just wheel her downstairs in front of the building. And from there they would watch the happenings of the neighborhood—greeting the neighbors and hearing the latest gossip. Betty enjoyed this for a time, but eventually, even this activity became too taxing. Finally she retreated to her apartment, not wanting to venture out at all. Betty had never been particularly fond of the wheelchair and she especially detested the walker that was provided for her. Debbie felt that her mother was unstable with the walker, finding it too difficult to coordinate her movements with the apparatus; and that was why she rarely relied on it. On the occasions that she did venture out, Betty would prefer to use a cane and Debbie's arm for support. She sometimes wondered why her body was so weak and unstable. Betty used to question whether or not exercise, earlier in her illness, would have kept her stronger. Twice during the course of her illness, she did receive physical therapy in her home and was able to practice some daily exercises that seemed to boost her stamina, both physically and emotionally. But Medicare will only cover a certain number of home health visits, as prescribed by the physician. So although Betty found these sessions helpful, they were unfortunately short-lived.

> Over the course of Betty's illness, can you recognize how decreased activity and mobility were indicators of her decline?

Betty often mentioned her best friend, Anna, in our phone conversations. They had been close friends for a long time. Less than two years before Betty got sick, Anna had come down with cancer herself. Betty was devastated when she learned of Anna's illness. She offered to go and clean house for her friend, which she did until Anna's death. But Anna would never talk about her cancer with Betty or what she was going through, and this was difficult for Betty. Since she never had the opportunity to speak openly with her friend, they were not able to grieve together. This silence was probably the most painful aspect for Betty in dealing with Anna's dying. I think it is a tribute to Betty that she did not follow those same footsteps. Although Betty was stricken with the same disease that took her friend, she *did* talk about her illness and about her feelings with those who were able to listen and support her.

Betty also talked about her dog Shu-Shu. He was a westie terrier who lived with Betty for 16 years before he finally had to be put down, just over a year before her illness was diagnosed. Shu-Shu was a beloved pet for Betty and she displayed his pictures in key places throughout the house. Whether she was talking on the phone, lying on the couch or napping in her bed, a picture of Shu-Shu was always close by for her to focus on. When I would ask Betty about her dreams she would mention dreaming either about Anna or Shu-Shu. Often during her nap times she would think of them and be comforted. Shu-Shu's ashes were placed in Betty's casket. They are close companions in death as they were in life.

In one of our phone conversations, Betty relayed stories to me about her childhood and family ties. In responding to my questions, she was able to review some of the significant events and people in her past—what they meant to her then and what they meant to her now. In one of the longest conversations we ever had, I was able to piece together many details about Betty's life and the pain she endured, even as a young child.

A volunteer can always be on the lookout for opportunities to explore, with the individual, pertinent details of their life history. Browsing through old photo albums together can provide a natural framework for these recollections. Conveying a sense of interest in the events that shaped this person's life reinforces her dignity and value. It may also help her gain a sense of closure and acceptance of situations that had previously remained beyond their ability to reconcile.

For the year that Betty was on the clinical trial drug, her condition stabilized. She gained back some of the weight she had lost during her radiation treatments, though Betty never did regain her sense of taste or enjoyment of food. As I mentioned, most of her pain was gone or at least tolerable, and for a time, she was able to resume some of her daily activities, like ironing, and assisting Debbie with the cooking and washing dishes. But her chronic depression never lifted; and although Debbie remembers many occasions when Betty was able to laugh and enjoy herself, her prevailing mood during that year was one of sadness and lethargy.

When discussing Betty's quality of life with Debbie, I once suggested they consider medications for depression and anxiety. It seemed to me that she might be able to better enjoy the life she had left if these symptoms could be treated. But neither Betty nor Debbie felt comfortable taking drugs unless it was absolutely necessary, and in this case, they felt it wasn't. In the same vein, I periodically suggested that Debbie consider receiving hospice services for her mother. Initially, Debbie was under the same misconception as many people, that hospice was simply a place where someone went to die. After I explained what hospice services were all about, as well as the criteria for receiving them, we realized that as long as Betty was participating in this clinical drug trial she would not be eligible.

However, I still felt that it would be helpful if a volunteer could come visit Betty maybe once or twice a week. This would allow Debbie to take some time away from her caregiving responsibilities while also enabling Betty to talk with someone who wasn't involved in the family dynamics. Debbie was not sure if her mother would go for this idea. Betty was not comfortable relying on strangers; the few times that Debbie suggested that maybe they should have someone come in during the day to help out, Betty had strongly vetoed the idea. Since this would be a volunteer situation, for only a couple of hours a week, Betty was willing to give it a try.

I linked Debbie up with a wonderful organization called "Compassion In Action," (listed in appendix). Volunteers are trained across the country to visit with the terminally ill. The central premise of CIA, whose chairman and founder is Dannion Brinkley, is that nobody should have to die alone. Although the main focus of the organization is veterans who are dying in VA hospitals, they will serve anyone with a terminal illness. Brinkley, author of *Saved by the Light*, was recently awarded the Silver Merit Award by the Veterans Administration Volunteer Service for over 8,750 hours spent at the bedside of dying veterans. In his hospice work, Dannion has cared for 348 people and spent a total of 16,473 hours at the bedside. This is what he says about his organization, taken from CIA's newsletter, volume 3, issue 4, 1999:

> We at Compassion in Action believe we are, in fact, our brothers' keepers and that every act of kindness has an impact far greater than its mere size. What we carry into the new millennium is an awareness of the dying process as a special and sacred time of life, a willingness to do the work to change America's consciousness about the end of life, and the concept of volunteers as the extended family of the future (p.1).

So a volunteer was assigned to visit Betty for a couple of hours and take her to the park. What happened in this case brought home a valuable lesson for me. Betty's volunteer was a high-powered attorney/business woman who seemed incredibly overextended in her life. She and Betty had a couple of visits and Betty took an interest in this woman's life. Apparently the volunteer was frantically searching for a place to move and nothing had turned up yet. I can understand that, given Betty's nurturing personality, she would have inquired about the volunteer's life. And I suppose it could be argued that in some instances it might be validating to encourage the expression of nurturing qualities, if that was a dominant, positive personality trait over the course of a lifetime, as it was in Betty's case. But, in this situation, even though this was her first assignment, I feel it was unprofessional of the volunteer to have allowed the conversation to focus solely on herself and her own needs. She was there to serve Betty and her primary responsibility, as a volunteer, was to listen. I believe it was on her second visit that she showed up over an hour late and on her third scheduled visit, she called to cancel. After that, Debbie and Betty decided it just wasn't working out and asked her not to come anymore.

Hearing the sequence of events, I was disappointed in how this volunteer handled herself. Perhaps she needed to get her life in order before taking on any future patients. This is an unfortunate scenario that can happen in any agency utilizing a volunteer pool, even one as fine and well respected as Compassion In Action. No matter how well someone is trained and how reputable the organization is that has trained them, occasionally a situation will arise that compromises these high standards. It is important for anyone taking on the compassionate care of the dying to realize that how an individual conducts himself when undergoing personal stress is pertinent to his ability to fulfill his responsibilities as a hospice volunteer. If someone is unable to keep his own counsel during difficult times, but instead shares his burdens indiscriminately with his patient, then he must step out of the situation. A discussion and evaluation between the volunteer and supervisor is recommended.

One of the things I find most remarkable about Betty's situation is the fact that, throughout the course of her illness, she required little, if any, pain medication. In her last days, she was receiving Percoset for pain, but in most instances, she could get by on Tylenol if need be. Debbie feels this is due in large part to her life-long avoidance of drugs and her high threshold for pain. Whatever the mitigating factors were, it certainly was a blessing for Betty that she did not need to be heavily medicated, as this would have only diminished her limited mental capacity, further compromising her quality of life. It makes me wonder whether her brain surgery and radiation may have short-circuited some of her pain pathways, because typically bone cancer can be excruciatingly painful.

In June of 2001, Betty's condition began to decline drastically. She had regular bouts of diarrhea, losing weight again and also losing strength. Betty was sleeping more during the day and having trouble sleeping through the night. She needed more round-the-clock care from Debbie, and as is predictable when only one person is handling all of the care, Debbie quickly wore herself out. Betty was still on the clinic trial drug, needing to have periodic checkups and tests. But these visits to the doctor were becoming more stressful as she was less and less able to handle them physically. Finally Debbie and her sister decided to take Betty off the drug. The diarrhea stopped almost immediately, but she continued to decline.

Betty was no longer awake to take my phone calls and she was barely eating. At this stage, Debbie was feeding her a few spoonfuls of oatmeal and water. Soon she was bed-bound and I suggested to Debbie that this might be the time to bring hospice in. It is often family or friends who first contact hospice on behalf of the patient. Without hesitation Betty's physician made the referral, and a hospice nurse came to the house for the assessment and paperwork.

Before long, Betty was refusing food altogether. This is an extremely painful threshold for most caregivers to cross with their loved ones. At this stage, especially after a long-term illness, as was Betty's, the primary caregiver's identity is almost totally defined by keeping their loved one alive and comfortable. If a patient stops eating, the message conveyed is that they are ready and wanting to die. Many caregivers are reluctant to accept this finality and begin to pressure their loved ones, subtly or not so subtly, to eat. Since we are conditioned that food is essential for life, we are hard pressed to witness someone deny herself in this way. It may seem as if she is trying to hasten her death, while those who love her may desperately want to slow it down. In Betty's case, she made her wishes very clear that she didn't want to eat, and Debbie, to her credit, was able to let that be.

> Can you describe the symptoms that marked Betty's transition into an active dying phase?

The last food Debbie fed her mother was a pureed peach, the day before she died.

Betty started receiving hospice care three weeks before she died, with the hospice nurse coming in once a week, primarily to check Betty's vital signs. Debbie's comment about the hospice experience was that it was "terrible." According to Debbie, they really didn't offer much of anything in terms of support or care either for Betty or for the family. Naturally, this assessment came as a disappointment to me. One can only assume that the agency who serviced them was understaffed; why else were there only three visits in a span of three weeks when Betty was so close to death? Why only a nurse visiting? Where were the social worker, the home health aide, the volunteer, and the chaplain? Sadly I am learning that the dying do not necessarily receive quality end-of-life care just because they are served by an agency that calls itself a hospice. Hospices will inevitably vary in quality across the board, regardless of demographics or non-profit/for-profit status.

Another sad reality is the average length of stay on hospice. According to a report issued by the National Hospice and Palliative Care Organization (NHPCO), in 2002 the average length of stay for over 800 hospices nationwide was 50.6 days. However, over a third of these patients received a week or less of hospice care. This figure has held stable since 2000 according to the report. There can be several reasons for this trend. As in Betty's case, outside resources can be viewed as more of a hindrance than a help.

Many people have misconceptions about hospice being a place to die rather than a holistic concept of care for the dying. As my local hospice literature states: "Affirming life, while recognizing that dying is a natural process, hospice care neither prolongs life nor hastens death. Hospice focuses on human values that go beyond the physical needs of the patient. In doing so, the hospice philosophy not only affirms the inherent dignity and worth of every individual, but also demonstrates the reverence of life in all stages." I think a significant reason why relatively few people have relied upon hospice's services or have done so only in their final days or even hours of life may be that physicians have been reluctant to refer their patients to hospice. Whether it is due to their own unresolved issues around death, or their view of hospice as "giving up" on their patients, or simply a lack of information about hospice services in general, physicians may experience difficulty in assisting their patients to transition from curative to comfort care.

The result is that patients often struggle with untreated pain as well as the side effects of futile curative treatments. Yes, these treatments may extend someone's life expectancy, but at what cost? I feel that post-poning hospice services until very little benefit can be gleaned from them is a reflection of our death-denying culture. Naturally it is not only physicians who are adversely affected by these cultural norms, but their patients as well. Even if a physician were to recognize that death was an inevitable outcome for a particular patient and want to make a referral to hospice, the individual may simply be unwilling to accept that outcome and will press on for further treatments. It is a complex issue, oftentimes revolving around an individual's right to hope, the physician's responsibility to respect that right, and the subtle differences between what constitutes true hope and false hope.

> As a reflective listener, how can the caregiver foster a sense of hope with the patient?

Jerome Groopman, M.D. recently wrote a remarkable book (listed in the appendix) on this topic: *The Anatomy of Hope, How People Prevail in the Course of Illness.* Groopman, a physician specializing in hematology and oncology, offers an array of stories about how hope or the lack of it had tremendous impact on the course of serious illnesses, both with himself and with his patients. Presenting thought-provoking examples of how crucial hope is to our overall well-being, Groopman maintains that: "We are just beginning to appreciate hope's reach and have not yet defined its limits. I see hope as the very heart of healing."

Betty died on a Friday afternoon. I had spoken on the phone with Debbie less than an hour earlier. We had been in touch several times those last couple of days, while I tried to support Debbie as well as I could from afar. I offered Debbie many suggestions for helping Betty have a peaceful and comfortable death. Betty was beginning to get a few bedsores, so I told Debbie how to treat them until the nurse could visit. I suggested using pillows and towels for helping to prop up Betty's fragile limbs, reminding her to turn Betty every couple of hours. I reassured her that bedsores are not uncommon, that it's simply the skin tissue breaking down as part of the dying process. I made sure that the nurse had left her some glycerin swabs to help keep Betty's mouth clean. Betty could also suck on this sponge for added moisture. Debbie's natural inclination was to keep the room dark and quiet. I also encouraged her to play some soft music, burn a candle with essential oils, such as lavender, and make whatever other changes to the room that would help create a comforting, peaceful atmosphere. When Debbie sponge-bathed her mother, she also massaged her with some of Betty's favorite lotion. Debbie often lay in bed with her mother, as she kept vigil day and night.

> How did Debbie make her mother more comfortable?

Debbie and her family had already made preliminary arrangements with a funeral home and cemetery. I explained that she didn't need to phone the funeral home immediately after Betty died. Once the hospice nurse had been called and the time of death noted, family members could sit quietly with Betty. I also encouraged Debbie to consider bathing and dressing her mother's body herself.

Most people don't ever consider that this is something they could do that would have great meaning for them and bring a sense of closure to the months and sometimes years spent caring for their loved one. We are culturally conditioned that once somebody dies, handling of the remains and all other preparations for the memorial and burial, are the responsibility of a mortuary. But of course, in generations prior to ours before the emergence of professional undertakers, family members and neighbors attended the dead. (See appendix for resources in caring for the dead.) Similarly, before the emergence of hospitals in our communities, people were born at home and usually died there as well. It's interesting to note that although most people state that their preference would be to die in the comfort and familiarity of their home, surrounded by loved ones, 56% of all deaths occurred in a hospital, according to the 1998 National Mortality Followback Survey, conducted by the CDC. And when in the hospital, it is not uncommon for patients, who are within hours or days of death, to receive significantly less contact from physicians, nurses and other hospital staff than patients who are ill but not terminal.

When we are healthy, we may hold an ideal of how we would like our death to be. But while in the grip of an end stage terminal illness, this picture radically changes and we are all too eager to retreat to a medical facility, believing that we will stay alive longer while receiving better care. I have no argument that the medical profession is proficient at prolonging life, but in the process it often overlooks how these interventions will impact the individual's quality of life. Does our pervasive fear of death lead us to choices that may extend our lives but radically diminish any joy or comfort in being alive? In letting go of curative treatments, can we actually extend our life expectancy as a result of receiving the specialized comfort-care that hospice provides?

> Have you thought about your own preferences with regard to dying? Have you completed a Living Will and Power of Attorney for Health Care?

In Betty's case, she was very clear that under no circumstances did she want to return to the hospital. Debbie felt confident in her ability to care for her mother at home, and Betty's death was such that her wishes were entirely honored.

Debbie was out in the living room on that Friday afternoon, visiting with her family. Her older sister was alone with Betty when Debbie heard a loud scream and then crying. She rushed into her mother's room and realized that her mother had just died. It does not surprise me that Betty passed when Debbie was out of the room. Often a death will occur when the person closest to the deceased has left the room—even just to go to the bathroom. People sometimes feel remorseful about not being present at the moment of death. The best explanation offered for this occurrence is that it may be easier, both for the one who is dying and for the loved one remaining, to sever the tie when the loved one is physically out of the room.

The sister was hysterical, so Debbie and her sister, Dawn, sent her out to be with the rest of the family. The room was quiet again, and Debbie later commented that a great sense of peace and light enveloped the room, tangible to both of them. Debbie and Dawn had planned to bathe and dress Betty themselves. They had previously selected her favorite dress and had on hand the towels, basin, and lotion they needed. After they had finished preparing their mother's body, they invited the other family members to come in.

Shortly thereafter, two men from the funeral home arrived. Debbie's comments were that they were gentle and respectful in handling Betty's body. She was particularly touched by how they placed Betty's head on a velvet pillow as they wheeled the body out of the apartment. Debbie and Dawn accompanied their mother's body out of the building. Several women who lived in the building and knew Betty were sitting outside on a bench, the same bench that Betty had sat on for so many hours herself. When the women saw Debbie, they knew it must be her mother's body on the cart. The women stood up silently as the body was wheeled past them. I felt tremendously moved by this gesture. To me it seemed like such a fitting and dignified salute to the friend and neighbor who had lived all of her adult life in that apartment building. Betty's life and memory will forever be emblazoned in the souls of all of us who loved her so dearly.

In a recent conversation with Debbie, several years following her mother's death, I asked her how she coped with the intensity of caring for Betty. "I received great satisfaction in taking care of my mother," Debbie replied. "It came naturally to me. But I also received a lot of emotional support from my family, who valued the commitment I made in being Betty's caregiver. To get out of the apartment for some exercise, I would run around the reservoir in Central Park. But mostly I prayed a lot and attended church services regularly. My faith gave me a lot of strength. Overall, it was as if my life contracted to just taking care of Betty. Now my life has expanded again, but you know, in some ways it was much simpler back then."

Misconceptions about Using Opioids to Treat Pain

Many individuals have concerns and sometimes misconceptions about the use of opioids (commonly referred to as narcotics) in treating pain. The two most prevalent fears on the part of patients and caregivers are that relying on opioids will lead to drug dependency and addiction, and that if one resorts to using opioids too early in the illness, as pain levels accelerate, the drugs will no longer be effective. Some physicians also have their own fears about prescribing opioids for pain management. The federal government has tight restrictions on the use of these substances, and although there are no federal regulations prohibiting opioid prescriptions for the purposes of palliative care in terminal cases, some doctors are still fearful of repercussions from the Drug Enforcement Administration (i.e. losing their license or reaping malpractice suits) for doing so. Much of this paranoia is the direct result of the extensive media coverage concerning Oxycontin, a long-acting synthetic form of morphine. Oxycontin has proven very effective in managing severe and chronic pain. However, it has also become the drug of choice for many substance abusers. So, although Oxycontin can be useful in alleviating pain and restoring quality of life, many patients are hesitant to use it because of the stigma associated with the drug.

In the audio documentary, *Heart-to-Heart: Caring for the Dying,* (included in appendix) the producer/director, Claire Schoen, comments that although it is a primary concern for health care providers and patients alike to insure satisfactory pain management at the end of life, recently there have been two different lawsuits brought against physicians in California for *under-medicating* and inadequately managing their dying patients' pain. According to Schoen, the California Medical Board found that the physicians were indeed negligent in both cases, and has subsequently mandated ongoing palliative care education for all physicians licensed by the state.

It is very unlikely that relying on opioids, most typically morphine, to alleviate pain in a terminal illness will lead to addictive behavior, especially when the patient is in the final stages of life. If the dosage and delivery are adequate to control the individual's pain, it is very rare to see the drug abuse behaviors and psychological dependence that characterize addiction. As far as tolerance levels for certain drugs are concerned, a physician skilled in palliative medicine will be able to prescribe medications based on regular and thorough assessments of the patient's symptoms and pain. For these reasons, a licensed pharmacist is a valuable member of the hospice team.

Keys for Creating Compassionate Care for the Dying

Weigh the odds. When considering ongoing treatment, it is important to weigh the benefits against the costs. Physicians focus on treatment options targeted at a specific disease but may overlook the cost of such treatments on the individual and her overall quality of life. In Betty's case, preparing for, traveling to and waiting long hours in the reception area for her doctor appointments was a hardship for her. Perhaps the ultimate significant success of the treatment in controlling Betty's pain made the arduous trips to her doctor appointments worthwhile.

Hold onto your doctor. When an individual is enrolled in hospice, the responsibility for medical care may be transferred from the patient's primary physician to the hospice physician. If there has been a long-standing patient/doctor relationship in place, losing a valuable support person at such a vulnerable time can be devastating. Some smaller hospices may encourage the patient's physician to remain involved in the case by conferring with the patient and attending IDT meetings as the doctor's schedule allows. While the long-standing doctor-patient relationship is important, competence in palliative care is equally important. If your physician does not possess these necessary skills, as many do not, it may be wise to have the hospice physician or another physician assume care responsibilities.

Ask for auxiliary services. Hospices vary in their approach to adjunct therapies. The hospice I work with supports various therapeutic interventions if they contribute to the patient's quality of life. For instance, we will send a physical therapist to help keep a patient ambulatory if he is engaged in activities around the home that enhance his sense of independence and enjoyment of life.

Report signs of extreme depression. Some depression is expected and appropriate in those who are dealing with a terminal illness. If the depression is severe and ongoing and interferes with the ability to continue living, the hospice team may make a psychiatric referral. In many instances, antidepressants have been successful in restoring a more balanced frame of mind.

Determine the pain threshold. Sometimes in order to think clearly and communicate effectively with loved ones, individuals choose to remain as lucid as possible during the last stages of their dying, even if it means tolerating a fair amount of pain and discomfort. Others overwhelmingly prefer to be "knocked out," finding comfort and peace through sedation. Understand the patient's goals in this regard to determine the best course of action.

Ask about common radiation side effects. When considering any course of treatment involving chemotherapy or radiation, be sure to ask the oncologist about all possible side effects. Also ask for a referral to a palliative care (pain relief) specialist so that any symptoms that are experienced can be well managed. Do not assume that oncologists or primary care physicians are trained in palliative medicine; often they are not. Please see Appendix A, "Relevant Terms," for a list of common radiation side effects.

Understand the hospice nurse's role. Though vital signs are taken as a baseline when a patient is first admitted onto hospice, it is uncommon to check them at each subsequent visit unless it is related to alleviating specific symptoms or anxiety. When visiting a patient, the first question a nurse might ask is, "What can I do for you today?" This invites the patient to communicate their needs first rather than having the nurse simply proceed with an agenda.

Pursue palliative care. Palliative care (treatment that focuses on alleviating pain or symptoms, while promoting better quality of care) can help those facing a serious illness cross the bridge into hospice care. Under current Medicare guidelines, certified hospices can only work with individuals who are no longer seeking a cure. Patients not yet ready to cease measures aimed at curing their condition can still reap the benefits of palliative care to diminish any unpleasant side effects they may have from their treatments. In this regard, palliative medicine is proving to be a vital link for making the transition into hospice. The following graph illustrates this progression of care from diagnosis through death. Bereavement care is available to loved ones through hospice for one year following the death.

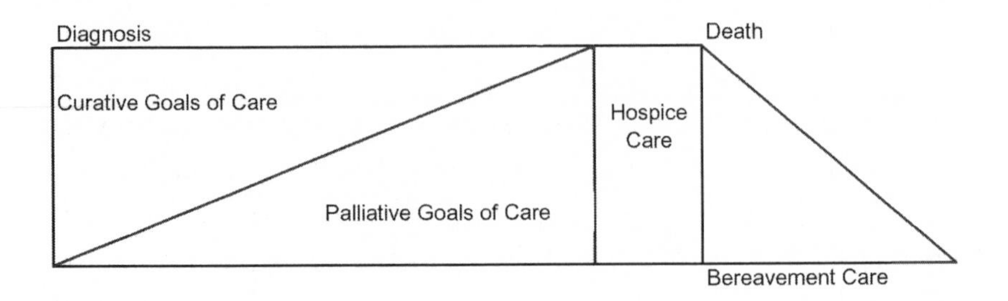

Dr. James Hallenbeck is medical director for the VA Hospice Care Center in Palo Alto, California, and has recently published a comprehensive book on the subject of palliative care entitled *Palliative Care Perspectives* (listed in Appendix B, "Selected Readings"). The text of his book can be viewed in its entirety at Growth House, Inc. at http://www.growthhouse.org/stanford.

Maintain oral hygiene. Oral hygiene is extremely important in helping keep the patient comfortable. Moist swabs can help relieve thirst, a common discomfort in end-stage dying. Maintaining oral hygiene also provides an excellent opportunity for the caregiver to check for signs of thrush, which can be painful for the patient. The symptoms of thrust are a sore mouth or throat or a white coating on the tongue. In most cases, thrush can be successfully treated with one or two doses of an antifungal pill if the patient is still able to swallow.

Name that tune. When choosing music to play during the active dying phase, carefully consider the individual's life-long musical preferences; they won't necessarily be soft or mellow! Gather this information ahead of time while helping the patient tie up loose ends. Playing music at this end stage of dying may serve the needs of the family and the "living" more than the needs of the dying. While some patients may be comforted by music, in this period of dissolution (dissolving into death) music is too "organized" and can be distracting.

Create compassionate care after death. Families may wish to sit with the body of a loved one for a period of time after the death. Even if the death has occurred outside the home, most professional staff will be respectful of these wishes. Suggestions for after-death care alternatives can be found in Appendix C, "Resources."

Keys for Self-Care

Respect the need to retreat. Withdrawing and assuming a predominantly passive role within the family structure can be a coping strategy for stress. It is not uncommon for husbands to respond in this way when faced with the loss of their spouses, especially if a daughter or son has stepped in as primary caregiver.

Keys for Hospice Volunteers

Take patients at face value. An advantage a volunteer may have over a friend or relative is that it is easier for volunteers to take the patient at face value. For example, although it can be beneficial to engage patients in previous favorite pastimes and hobbies, some patients may no longer be interested in or have the energy for these pursuits. Yet some patients may take the path of least resistance by acquiescing to their family's assumptions and needs in deference to their own desires. If you notice the family placing undue pressure on the patient to fulfill previous roles, bring this information back to the hospice team. It may be appropriate for the social worker to intervene.

9

CREATING A NEW LIFE

Peg and Marty lived in my neighborhood. Peg was suffering from Parkinson's disease and a seizure disorder. She also had advanced dementia, probably the result of the seizures. Healthy most of her life, her illness came on suddenly and advanced rapidly. Peg was 77 years old. Her husband, Marty, was her primary caregiver. They'd been married for many years and had raised a large family together.

Marty greeted me at the door and immediately struck me as warm and welcoming. We shook hands and then he led me into Peg's room. Peg and Marty were practicing Catholics and there were holy pictures throughout the house, especially in Peg's bedroom. Until quite recently Peg and Marty slept together in the same bedroom where they had slept for most of their married life. But Peg had taken several bad falls when trying to get up during the night, and for her safety a hospital bed with guardrails was put in the guest bedroom.

Peg was sleeping and seemed to be comfortable. Marty explained to me that she slept almost continuously now. She was mostly bedridden, though Marty would put her in a wheelchair and take her to the living room when their children and grandchildren were visiting. Peg seemed to thoroughly enjoy these visits from her family and it was really the only time she seemed responsive to those in her environment. Marty went through great pains to prepare food for his wife. He used a blender to puree all sorts of different nutritional drinks (made from vegetables and fruits), which he then would spoon-feed to Peg. She would eat very little, but that didn't discourage Marty. He was a soft-spoken man whose presence was nurturing and loving. When he spoke about his wife, it was with the greatest tenderness and respect. I was moved at how much he still loved her and how committed he was in caring for her. I was called in as a volunteer to relieve Marty for a few hours every week so that he could leave the house and do some chores.

> How can a volunteer gather information about a person's life without relying on verbal communication?

I probably made four or five visits to see Peg. Only once during my time with her did she make eye contact and smile at me. Most of the time she slept. Sometimes I would stroke her head and quietly talk to her. Sometimes I would recite some Catholic prayers that I remembered from childhood. Sometimes I read to her from her devotional magazine. Sometimes I sat quietly by her bed, meditating and listening to her breathing. And occasionally I would read to her from the book I was reading at the time. I always work on the premise that the patient can hear me, even when sleeping or in a coma.

This case was unique for me in that Peg was the only hospice patient I had ever visited who never spoke to me. In tangible ways, our relationship was therefore limited. But I trust that we did connect on levels that were important to both of us. Loving someone is not dependent on words or other easily identifiable gestures. It's like loving an infant—you just do it!

In contrast to Peg, conversations with Marty flowed easily. He told me about his work as a general contractor. Now, one of his sons was carrying on in the trade and, of course, Marty was pleased about that. He shared details about his other children, where they lived and what they were doing. Marty spoke about years gone by, how Peg loved her kids and what a terrific mother she was. He smiled as he remembered how eager she was to invite friends over for dinner. Never intimidated about what to serve her company, Peg was a pro at pulling together whatever was on hand. She especially loved to bake and always had treats on the table for family and friends. I noticed a wedding picture on the wall, with two couples in it. Marty explained that Peg was a twin and that her sister had married his brother—they had a double wedding! Now how often do you hear about something like that happening? Several of our conversations went on along these lines. It was almost as if Marty was doing a life review on behalf of his wife.

During my last visit with Peg, it was clear that she would die very soon. The hospice nurse advised Marty to stop feeding her because she was no longer swallowing effectively. The food was just caking on her tongue and inside her mouth. It was also very likely that Peg could choke. Her breathing was becoming shallow and irregular, with long pauses between the breaths. The next day was one of their sons' birthday and Marty was concerned that Peg's death might fall on that day. However, he also realized that it was out of his hands and there was no use fretting over it. When it was time to leave, I kissed Peg gently on her forehead and squeezed Marty's arm. I received a phone call two days later saying that Peg had died—the day after her son's birthday!

I did not attend her funeral, but the following week I called Marty and set up a time to visit. We sat on the couch in the living room, while he told me all about the funeral and the many condolences he and his family received. I asked him about Peg's death, and he said she died peacefully with several of their children around her. After a while we talked about his plans for the future. Marty told me he was planning to put some finishing touches on his motor home and take to the road. He showed me the motor home and explained what still needed work. Marty said he would put the house on the market next spring as he hoped to spend the next few years traveling. I was impressed by his courage—his abil-

> How does Peg and Marty's story illustrate the concept that how we die often reflects how we have lived?

ity to look toward the future. He no doubt grieved the loss of his lifelong partner, but he also realized that he had to go on and that there was still a lot of life left to enjoy. I gave him a big hug when I left and wished him all the best.

I ran into Marty the following autumn at a community event. We gave each other a hug; it was so crowded and noisy we really couldn't stop to talk. But I have learned of some news about Marty through another connection. I was speaking to our office manager about my hospice work and she mentioned that she had a good friend whose mother had been on hospice. Her friend spoke very highly of the hospice team. I asked our manager the mother's name and, sure enough, it was Peg! She went on to tell me that Marty had met someone from a neighboring city, moved there and was recently married. I was glad to hear this news and that Marty had found someone to share his future with. He took such wonderful care of Peg; I hope his new wife will do the same for him.

Keys for Creating Compassionate Care for the Dying

Assume the patient is always listening. Of our five senses, hearing and touch are typically the last to go. If a patient has been unresponsive—sleeping for long stretches or in a coma—it's easy to assume that they are "someplace else" and aren't aware of what is going on around them. Though they may not be able to respond, they can hear what's being said and can benefit from any loving, physical contact. Continue to talk, to read, to sing, to pray, to touch—carry on with whatever communication feels most comforting. Likewise, if you need to relay information about the patient that you wouldn't want them to hear, be mindful of this and step out of the room.

Keys for Hospice Volunteers

Take care of the caregiver. Hospice volunteers are trained to provide comfort not only for patients but for caregivers as well. If the patient is comatose or sleeping during your visits, you may find that you have more meaningful interactions with the caregiver than the patient. When you are caring for the caregiver, you can use many of the same compassionate principles you use in caring for the patient. Be fully present and listen attentively no matter what the person's role is.

Establish closure with the caregiver. Attending memorial services or viewing the body can be good ways to establish closure with your patients who have passed on, but what about establishing closure with the caregiver? If you have formed a friendship with the caregiver and would like to visit her after a death, inform the bereavement coordinator so this can be incorporated into the plan of care. In some hospices, volunteers regularly participate in the bereavement program.

10

AFTER-DEATH CARE

At church one Sunday, a woman named Susan approached me, asking about hospice. Susan and her sister, Jane, were caring for their mother. Susan said that they were both on the brink of exhaustion from their caregiving duties. Becky Sue, their mother, had suffered a series of strokes and her condition had deteriorated rapidly in the last few weeks. In recent days, she had required continual care and Susan didn't know how much longer she could handle it. She wanted information about hospice, so I explained the two criteria for eligibility: as determined by the patient's primary physician and the hospice medical director, the individual has a six months or less life expectancy and is not pursuing any further curative or life prolonging treatments. She said her mother fit these criteria and asked how she could get her mother signed on. I gave her the hospice manager's name and phone number, explaining that she would need a referral from Becky's physician. Susan thanked me for my help and I wished her luck.

As it turned out, I was filling in as temporary volunteer coordinator during this time and when I went into the office the following week, I saw that I was given a new patient who needed volunteer services—none other than Becky Sue! Because my work hours were taken up with extra duties, I was not able to see any patients. I looked through the volunteer list and called Ellen to see if she'd be available. It turned out that Ellen was an acquaintance of Susan's from several years ago, although they had not recently been in touch. Ellen shared with me that she wanted to take this case on, but was concerned about how she would handle herself with Susan. Although their relationship had primarily been good, Ellen said that she had experienced some boundary issues with Susan and didn't know if they would come up again. I explained that if she decided to take this case, she'd be going into the home as a hospice volunteer, not as a personal friend. She would need to explain this to Susan. I reminded her not to give Susan her home phone number and that if Susan needed to get a message to Ellen, it would have to go through the office or myself. I encouraged Ellen to give it a try and told her not to hesitate to call me if anything came up.

When I followed up with Ellen to see how the first visit went, she sounded very enthusiastic. She had hit it off with Becky Sue and was also enjoying getting acquainted with her husband as well. Susan was thrilled to have Ellen as the volunteer, and at least for the time being, no complications arose from their previous relationship. Ellen went on visiting Becky Sue for a number of weeks. Just after Christmas I received a call from Ellen telling me that she'd be going out of town over New Year's. It was expected that Becky wouldn't live much longer. Ellen went on to tell me that after the death, Susan and Jane were planning to keep their mother's body at home for 48 hours, before taking it to the family farm, several hours away, for burial. The sisters were planning to bathe and dress their mother, then keeping the body iced down, allow friends and family to hold a vigil by the body. I knew that our hospice had probably not encountered such a situation before and I was curious as to how our nurses would respond. Since Ellen would probably not be back in time to participate in the vigil, I told her that I would be honored to sit in her place.

At the following IDT meeting, we discussed the situation. Though initially a little startled by the idea, the nurse assigned to Becky Sue's case was entirely supportive of the family's wishes. We had a brief discussion as to whether or not this matter had been cleared with the coroner's office. The nurse said she would talk with Susan and make sure that this not-so-minor detail had been covered. Meanwhile, the nurses agreed that whoever was on call would help the sisters bathe and dress the body.

That afternoon I called Susan and she told me that she had spoken with the nurse, assuring her that everything was taken care of. The coroner had been over to meet with Susan, and as long as the body was sufficiently iced and the room kept chilled, he saw no reason why the body could not remain in the house for two days. However, he did advise her that if kept much longer than that, the body would start decomposing. Susan had done her homework; she contacted *Crossings*, a resource center for after-death care. Committed to transforming society's attitudes and behaviors at the time of death, *Crossings* (included in the appendix) educates families on how to act as funeral directors—legal in 45 states. They provided Susan with the practical tools that enabled Susan to feel confident for caring for her mother after death.

Susan knew that Ellen was going to be away, so I asked her if I could participate in the vigil on her behalf. Susan was very pleased and asked me to come over the following day, so I could meet Becky Sue before she died.

Susan and her husband lived in the house where she had grown up. In fact, as a little girl she remembers her mother caring for Susan's grandmother as she was dying. So this house held a lot of memories for her. When I arrived, Susan immediately took me upstairs to her mother's room. I noticed the chairlift on the stairway, and Susan said she had it installed after her mother's hip surgery when she could no longer negotiate the steep stairway. Quietly we entered Becky Sue's room. Susan's sister Jane was sitting by the bed, talking to her mother. Susan introduced me to Jane and to Becky Sue, then they both left so we could get acquainted. Becky Sue's voice was very soft; I had to lean in close to her in order to make out what she was saying. Her dementia was significant and the things she said didn't make sense from what I could sort out. Periodically, family members would come and visit for a few minutes—her granddaughter and son had spent several days visiting and were now preparing to leave. The granddaughter read a story to Becky Sue and then played a few tunes on an auto harp, before kissing her grandmother goodbye.

After their departure, the house seemed to quiet down a little. A long stretch of companionable silence had passed when Becky Sue started talking about a train ride, wondering when the train was going to get in. She said that there would be two children on the train accompanying her. My ears perked up as I recognized that she was speaking in metaphor about her dying. She was concerned about crossing a bridge to meet the train, and I assured her that she would receive all the help she needed. I told Becky Sue how excited and happy I was for her as she prepared for her journey, and then she gently closed her eyes and fell asleep. I quietly gathered my belongings and tiptoed out of her room.

> Can you recall an instance when a patient or loved one may have been speaking in metaphor regarding the circumstances or timing of his death?

When I shared her mother's train vignette with Susan, and how common these travel stories are among the dying, she was excited and promptly copied it down in her journal. Susan said that over the past week, tucked inside incoherent ramblings, her mother had made a couple of direct comments about dying and death. Becky Sue seemed to have no fears about what lay ahead.

Several days passed and Becky Sue was still with us. This was one of those instances when nobody could figure out why. According to the nurse's account, all physical signs indicated that her body was shutting down. With all their combined years of experience in hospice, our nurses are still amazed at how far off they can be in anticipating a patient's death. Becky Sue knew the train schedule; the rest of us could only guess!

In the predawn hours on Sunday morning, Becky Sue left this world gently, with her son by her side. Susan immediately put in a call to a friend whose job it was to collect the ice. Ben got in his van and drove to one of the local, all night supermarkets. When he asked one of the clerks for 50 lbs of ice, at two o'clock in the morning no less, Ben hoped he wouldn't have to answer the obvious question. I wonder if he had been asked what he was planning to do with all that ice, whether or not he would have told the truth. Meanwhile, the hospice nurse had been called and soon came over to help the sisters bathe and dress their mother's body.

I received word of Becky Sue's passing at church the following morning. I went over to sit with the body that afternoon. Susan and Jane had transformed their mother's room. When I was there a few days ago, sleeping bags, blankets and pillows were strewn on the floor where different family members had slept. As with any sick room, it easily became cluttered. But today, the room was tidy. A small altar was prepared with favorite family pictures and flowers. Essential oils were burning as well as candles. Becky Sue's body was beautifully laid out, her head wrapped in a lovely purple babushka. Her hands were holding a white rose. The bags of ice had been wrapped in towels, tucked alongside the body and hidden by the sheets. Becky Sue looked radiant and it was a joy to join the others praying, singing, reading and meditating around her body. The vigil continued all through Sunday and into Monday morning. On Monday afternoon, the family held the celebration service in their living room, while the body remained upstairs. There were poetry and scripture readings, piano and violin music, dancing and singing. It was truly a festival of love. I am so glad that I had the chance to meet Becky Sue during her final days of life and to participate in the vigil and celebration honoring her. And I am also glad that Susan and Jane had the desire and commitment to take care of their mother, both in life and in death—to do what was once so commonplace for families many years ago.

> What are some of the benefits for the family in caring for their dead? How can this practice help change our culture's perception of death?

Keys for Creating Compassionate Care for the Dying

Find out about after-death care. After a death, a family may wish to care for and be with their loved one. They may, for instance, want to sit with the body of a loved one for a period of time after the death. Even if the death has occurred outside the home, most professional staff will be respectful of these wishes. *Crossings* is an excellent resource center to learn about after-death care alternatives, focusing on educating families to act as funeral directors, which is legal in 45 states. *Crossings* is committed to transforming society's attitudes and behaviors at the time of death. For more information, you may contact them at http://www.crossings.net.

Keys for Self-Care

Don't let the stress get you down. Many studies now indicate that caregivers are especially susceptible to illness due to heightened levels of stress. In a population-based study of 400 in-home caregivers plus 400 controls published in the *Journal of the American Medical Association* (1999), caregivers reporting emotional strain had an increased risk of death and a substantial increased risk of major depression. A similar study published in the *American Journal of Preventive Medicine* (2003) studied a pool of 54,412 nurses and found that those who cared for an ill spouse for more than nine hours per week had an increased risk of heart attacks or cardiac death. To ensure that you don't become one of these statistics, take care of yourself *before* you care for anyone else. Get plenty of rest, eat balanced meals, get out of the house for some fresh air and exercise, check out a caregiver support group and pick up the phone and call some friends. If you are struggling to keep up and are feeling overwhelmed, ask your friends for help. Or better yet, call the hospice office and ask them to send over a volunteer!

11

LET IT BE

The minister at my church phoned me one day to ask for help. Besides his duties as minister, Peter also held the position of Spiritual Care Coordinator for the hospice program. He explained that he had recently been visiting a young man, Doug, who was currently undergoing cancer treatments. The social worker at the hospital's cancer treatment center had asked him to visit with Doug because he seemed to be struggling with spiritual issues related to his illness. The social worker felt that Peter would be able to address Doug's concerns. Doug was not a hospice patient at this point because he was still receiving curative treatments, so Peter was not wearing his hospice hat during these visits, but simply volunteering his own time to support Doug. The reason he was seeking my help was that Doug had recently spent a couple of weeks in the hospital, recovering from severe side effects from his treatments. Doug was due to be released in the next day or so and his girlfriend, Cynthia, had asked Peter if he knew of anyone that might be able to sit with Doug for a few hours a week while she was working. And Peter thought of me. Peter realized that he first needed to clear this with the hospice manager, before asking a hospice volunteer to take on a patient.

The manager explained that just as Peter was seeing Doug strictly as a community spiritual leader and not in any official hospice capacity, the same would hold true for me—I would be visiting Doug as a member of Peter's church community, not as a hospice volunteer. If Doug eventually enrolled in hospice, I would simply continue on in this role so as not to create any confusion for him. Provided I was clear about these parameters, the hospice manager had no reservations about my involvement in the case. Peter gave me a few more details about Doug and Cynthia's situation as well as their phone number. I told him I would call them and set up a visiting schedule. I also asked that Peter keep in touch about any pertinent developments in Doug's care.

I left a message on their answering machine and Cynthia called back the following day. She explained that Doug's favorite pastime these days was watching movies or television, and she was hoping just to have a companion for Doug at least some of the time during her absence. We set up a tentative schedule of two mornings per week, consisting of two hours each visit. I remember feeling especially cautious in covering my bases with Cynthia. Questions such as: was Doug ambulatory, would he need assistance to the bathroom, was there a number posted where I could reach her? I was used to receiving information like this before visiting a new patient and I wanted to be somewhat prepared for whatever his needs might be. I told Cynthia I was looking forward to meeting Doug and hoped that she and I would someday have the opportunity to meet as well. Thus concluded the only conversation we would ever have.

It was August and Doug lived only a few blocks from my home, so once again I was fortunate to be able to ride my bike to these visits. I knocked on the door and waited for a call to come in, as I knew he'd be expecting me. Instead, Doug labored out of his recliner to answer the door himself, and after seeing how much this effort exhausted him, I vowed silently to always let myself in after knocking in the future. Doug was a young man in his early thirties, the youngest patient I've ever visited. He had all the features one comes to expect in a cancer patient—a bald head, an emaciated body, and penetrating eyes. My first impression of their living room was how clean and peaceful it seemed. Sick rooms can easily amass clutter and smells, which become invisible to the patient and caregiver, but are at once noticeable to a visitor. Instead of used tissues, dirty glasses and plates and random medicinal items, I noticed candles, pictures of nature, cards from friends, and other valued possessions lovingly arranged in different locations around the room. The effect was calming, almost sacred.

After settling ourselves down in our respective seats, I started up the first of what ultimately turned out to be several aborted attempts at conversation with Doug. The television was on and I noticed that Doug did not turn down the volume upon my arrival. I asked him how he was feeling today and he said he was not doing that great. Doug asked me how I knew Peter, so I explained our connection. Doug then asked me how long I'd been a volunteer with hospice and how many patients I had visited during that time. After answering these brief, introductory queries, Doug's attention riveted back to the television screen, as he started to fuss with the reception. Once he got a relatively clear picture, he then placed his full attention on the talk show he had selected and I sensed that any further conversation would not be well received. And that became the predictable pattern of all our visits—maybe five to ten minutes of conversation couched between "Live with Regis and Kelly," "Martha Stewart" and "Family Feud." I am not a television watcher—I don't even own one—so I found it particularly frustrating to be watching morning TV when I would have preferred getting to know this man sitting beside me. I was reminded of my time with James at the hospital, when he would withdraw into the television and how frustrated I would feel over the distance it put between us.

But visiting with someone who is critically ill, and possibly dying, is not about meeting my needs and preferences, and I would constantly come back to this simple fact. Still, I harbored lingering doubts that maybe I was not trying hard enough to engage Doug in conversation. I wondered if it was a fear that nudging him into an active dialogue, and possibly getting

> How do you establish rapport with a new patient?

rebuffed, made me reticent to intrude upon his mesmerism with the TV. Based on my layperson's observations, Doug came across as depressed and utterly enervated from his cancer. Under these circumstances, perhaps watching movies and television was his chosen coping mechanism. Whatever the "right answer" was, the question certainly worked me continuously during my brief span of visits (five) with Doug. But we did have a couple of significant exchanges between us, which stand out in my memory during those late summer mornings.

I asked Doug if he would share with me some background concerning his illness. He told me that he moved to Montana from Oregon only a few years ago to enroll in a psychology/business graduate program at the university. Cynthia, his longtime girlfriend, accompanied him in the move. Within months of their arrival, Doug's health started mysteriously deteriorating. Prior to this, Doug said his health and stamina had always been excellent. At first he described feeling flu-like symptoms that seemed to linger on and on. As these intensified, he was no longer able to keep up with his classes and daily routine. Doug contacted a physician and underwent a battery of tests. The gist of the story, as I understood it, was that initially the doctor could not isolate the cause of Doug's elevated white cell count and his obviously compromised immune system. It took months to diagnosis a very rare type of cancer, which by this time had metastasized to other organs. Doug underwent aggressive chemotherapy and radiation treatments, which ravaged his already exhausted body. It was after one of these rounds, when Doug was admitted into the hospital to stabilize the severe side effects, that he was first introduced to Peter.

I was aware that Doug was in a holding pattern, waiting to see if his latest treatment protocol was going to be successful. I knew he would be receiving some news by the time of my next visit, so when I returned later that week, I asked Doug what he had learned from his doctor. He looked me straight in the eye, saying that there was no improvement and that the doctor had nothing else to offer. I held his gaze and told him how sorry I felt, and that I could not imagine how he must have received that news. I believe that moment was the most authentic and intimate one we shared. After some silence, I said it seemed that this news catapulted him to yet another juncture in dealing with his illness, so I asked him if he would share his feelings about that with me. Doug said that he was afraid. When I asked what he was most afraid of, he replied that he had no concept of what would happen to him after he died, and that basically terrified him. Doug explained that he had been working on these issues with Peter, but he still had not broken through to find any satisfying answers or peace for himself.

I asked him about hospice and whether or not his physician had mentioned this as a possible next step. He said no, there was no discussion about it. Frankly, I was stunned. I knew who his oncologist was, and ironically, this person had been the hospice physician for several years. Perhaps the doctor felt that Doug needed more time to come to terms with his terminal diagnosis before taking the next step. Since I brought up the idea of hospice, Doug proceeded to ask me exactly what hospice was. I explained that it was a holistic system of care, delivered by a team of professionals and volunteers, whose purpose was to provide comprehensive care for individuals with terminal illnesses, as well as support for their caregivers. I gave a brief overview of the various team members and their roles as well as the current eligibility criteria for receiving these services. Doug seemed satisfied with my answers and then turned his attention back to the television.

In preparation for what turned out to be my last visit with Doug, I inventoried my books about death and dying and selected one to lend to Cynthia and Doug. The book, *To Live Until We Say Goodbye* with photographs by Mal Warshaw and text by Elisabeth Kubler-Ross, M.D. is a photo journal of several individuals with end-stage cancer. It offers an up-close and honest accounting of how these individuals approached their dying with the support of Dr. Kubler-Ross. I selected this book to loan to Doug and Cynthia because I felt the photographs and stories were exceptionally candid; I was hoping that this might help Doug better see his own reflection and find his way through this painful transition of clinging to life while preparing for death.

I was nervous showing him the book. My anguish was about whether I might be promoting my own agenda and overstepping my boundaries in offering him this material. In the end, I just explained briefly what it was about, how it was formatted and why I liked it so much. Then, I left it on the coffee table and said goodbye. I reasoned that Doug wouldn't have to even open the book if he felt it was out of his league. Even if he chose not to look at it, Cynthia might find some value in it for herself.

> Doug's story illustrates the struggle a volunteer may experience between "doing"and "being." How is this struggle depicted?

Peter phoned me a few days later to explain that Doug's mother would soon be arriving in town. Doug had asked Peter to convey to me how appreciative he was of my spending time with him, and requested that I not come over for the time being, since his mother was visiting. Peter didn't know how long she would be staying, so in turn, I didn't know when, or even if, I'd ever see Doug again. The seemingly abrupt manner in which my visits had been discontinued was hard for me to deal with at first. Though I completely understood and supported Doug's need for privacy with his mother, I felt at loose ends in our all too brief relationship. Establishing some sense of closure with the folks I visit has always been an important aspect for me in my hospice work. Maybe my leaving the book for him, offering Doug this final gift of my caring, was indeed an act of closure, although unbeknownst to me at the time.

I never did see Doug again. He eventually signed onto hospice, but declined to have any volunteers come over as he was receiving adequate support from friends and family. I received news of his death in early December. In a hospice team debriefing, I learned that he never did come to terms with his anxiety over death, and what he perceived to be the haunting void beyond. I can only pray that in spite of his open-ended struggles, Doug's soul will continue the search—the learning and the lessons—wherever his ongoing journey takes him.

Keys for Creating Compassionate Care for the Dying

Be authentic. When sharing a patient's grief, be honest and authentic. Even a response such as "I don't know what to say" is an honest way of conveying empathy and support.

Ask about palliative sedation. When all attempts at treating unendurable symptoms (such as severe anxiety) in a dying patient have failed, palliative sedation may be an appropriate alternative. *The Hospice and Palliative Nurses Association* (listed in Appendix C, "Resources") defines palliative sedation as "the monitored use of medications intended to induce varying degrees of unconsciousness, but not death, for relief of refractory and unendurable symptoms in imminently dying patients." From an ethical and legal standpoint, it is important to distinguish the difference between euthanasia and palliative sedation. The End of Life/Palliative Education Resource Center (EPERC) identifies intent as the key difference between the two: "In euthanasia, the intent is to produce a hastened death. In sedation, the intent is to relieve intractable suffering, not hasten death." (See http://www.eperc.mcw.edu/ff_index.htm, Fast Fact #106.) This definition is compatible with hospice's philosophy to neither hasten death nor prolong suffering. If needed, families and patients can ask the palliative care specialist to carefully review with them the option of sedation.

Keys for Hospice Volunteers

Leave your agenda at the door. It can be difficult for volunteers to leave their agendas at the front door, especially when meeting a patient for the first time. We want the visit to go well, and even that is an expectation that could interfere with the needs of the patient. Visiting with someone who is critically ill and possibly dying is not about meeting our needs and preferences but theirs. For example, as volunteers, how do we define a "good visit"? For me, it used to mean establishing some kind of connection with the individual. Yet, as in Doug's case, patients don't always share that same need and may focus primarily on the television as their way of coping. In cases like this, don't feel the need to press them into conversation. I have now come to define a good visit as being open to whatever unfolds, allowing the patient to be as he is without placing judgment on either of us.

Rely on your team for support. If you have questions or concerns about how you are getting along with your patient, don't hesitate to discuss your experience with the volunteer coordinator. He may be able to offer you some background information that will bring greater clarity to the situation, helping you to find a better way of relating.

Let the patient take the lead. When in doubt about the appropriateness of pursuing some course of action, it may be best to err on the side of caution, if there isn't anyone inside the situation to consult. Take your cue from the patient. For example, if she doesn't seem to be comfortable discussing the topic of death, you don't have to feel compelled to go there. In a conversation with the hospice manager, I was told that Doug had indeed felt uncomfortable with my efforts to broach the topic of dying, and this was the reason I was not asked to come back. But since Doug was not enrolled in hospice during the course of my visits, I had to simply rely on my own judgment. Doug was utilizing the television as his primary coping mechanism and did not desire much conversation with me. If I could have truly accepted this, there would have been no need to press him to engage in conversation.

12

SECOND-HAND SMOKE

It was early November when I first visited Vivian at the nursing home. I was assigned to her case by the new volunteer coordinator for the hospice office. When filling out the form detailing my available hours and volunteer preferences, I had indicated that I did not want to be placed in the home of a patient who smoked. I had grown up in a small apartment with my mother smoking cigarettes and my father smoking a pipe—both my parents are still alive and both have quit their habits because of troubling health-related symptoms. I figured my lungs had absorbed enough second-hand smoke for a lifetime. Vivian was a two-pack a day gal before her diagnosis of breast cancer, which had subsequently metastasized to her brain, and saw no point in changing her ways now. Technically, patients are not allowed to smoke in nursing homes, but why would Vivian be bothered by such trivial rules? Vivian was a headstrong woman in her fifties and didn't ask to be placed in the nursing home by her case worker and doctors (She had been enrolled in welfare services for many years). However, once she was caught in the act, the nursing home staff confiscated her smokes and kept them under lock and key at the nurses' station. Vivian could go outside for a cigarette, but there would be no more smoking escapades in her room.

So my services were enlisted twice a week to accompany her outside while Vivian lit up. I imagine Vivian was able to get outside on her own most of the time, with some assistance from the staff with elevator transport, opening doors, etc. because she was in a wheelchair. The hospice team concurred that Vivian would benefit from some one-on-one companionship and Vivian was amenable to this idea as well. Despite my strong aversion to second-hand smoke, I decided to take on the case. I rationalized that we would be outside and that I could stay out of the way of most of the smoke. Ahh, well. Sometimes my strategy worked, and sometimes I got a good hit of it in my face. But the benefits of sharing this brief time with Vivian far outweighed the little discomfort I experienced.

I was somewhat stunned when I first saw her as she bore an amazing resemblance to my mother. They were both small in stature with the same prominent chin and high forehead. Both wore glasses and had receding hairlines with very thin hair. My mother is almost thirty years older than Vivian, but because of the ravages of cancer, their predominant features were hauntingly similar. A trait that was not at all similar was the level of volume in their voices. My mother has been deaf for many years, so she experiences great difficulty modulating her voice, which often results in her shouting more often than talking. Vivian's voice hardly registered above a whisper so it took great concentration to follow her in a conversation. And finally, of course, there was their shared affinity for smoking. My mother quit eight years ago after undergoing triple bypass surgery for her second heart attack. This was long after I had moved out of the apartment, so most of my memories of living with my mother factor in her smoking.

It seems I felt a fairly strong personal connection with Vivian right from the start. Our visits were predictable in that shortly after my arrival, Vivian would bundle herself up in hat, coat and scarf with a blanket tucked around her legs, and we would head down to the nurses' station to collect her cigarettes and lighter. Once outside, I would settle myself on the bench while Vivian lit up. She explained how difficult it was for her to come to terms with her smoking since living at the nursing home. She felt that, overall, the staff was very critical and resistant to her smoking and this caused her significant self-doubt and concern. During my visits, I did not observe any of the staff treating Vivian disrespectfully or in any other way trying to curtail her smoking outside. In fact, I often found various staff sharing their cigarette breaks with her. It finally dawned on me to check for Vivian at the rear entrance where most of the staff congregated to smoke, before trekking upstairs to her room. But then again, the nurses did keep close tabs on her cigarettes and lighter; perhaps having to ask for and then surrender them after each outdoor smoke felt degrading and prohibitive to Vivian.

Her other issue concerning smoking focused on the severity of her illness and her lack of ability to quit. Vivian the cancer had advanced and that her dying was imminent. Whereas many people in similar straits would indulge freely in their vices, supported by the rationale that since they were dying anyway they might as well enjoy themselves to the end, Vivian was struggling with other considerations. She sometimes chided herself for not having the discipline and determination to give up smoking, as she thought that was the preferred course, and certainly it was what others expected of her, or so she thought. By the same token, Vivian realized that the nicotine helped calm her down and, to some extent, smooth over her worries. Because of this, she felt cigarettes were an essential crutch for her right now. I don't know if she ever came to peace with the issue, but I do know she continued to smoke right up until the day she went into a coma.

> How does a life-long addiction take on new significance after a terminal diagnosis?

Vivian made frequent comments about her faith in God and how He had always looked out for her throughout her life. She sometimes worried about how the events in her immediate future were going to play themselves out. Vivian had unpaid bills piling up at her apartment, worry number one. Her other concern was how long she was going to need to remain at the nursing home. Because of her advancing dementia, it was sometimes difficult to assess just how much information about her situation Vivian was able to comprehend and retain. Since I could not address the status of her bills or nursing home stay, I tried to reconnect her to her faith, while encouraging Vivian to turn her concerns over to God. This approach always seemed to comfort and reassure her. We would laugh about the idea that she might not have a damn clue what any of this was all about, but God certainly would sort it all out in good time.

I think our most special visit together was when I wheeled her a few blocks to the downtown area and we strolled up and down the sidewalks, marveling at the newly designed window displays for Christmas. Vivian and I were like two young children as we gazed in wonder at all the various holiday scenes. What seemed to touch Vivian's heart most deeply was the beautifully depicted nativity scene in one particular shop window. Vivian was relieved that amidst all the secular and commercial trappings of Christmas, at least one business owner decided to honor the spiritual origins of this holiday. During that early Christmas stroll, there was no way for us to know that this would be Vivian's final recognition of Christmas before her death.

> How did Vivian's smoking exacerbate her feelings of isolation? How did it facilitate companionship?

The following week when I arrived at the nursing home, I stopped in at the nurses' station and learned that Vivian had taken a sudden downturn. She was floating in and out of consciousness, her extremities were bluish and cold to touch, and in the past 24 hours she had taken neither food nor liquids. By all appearances, Vivian was actively dying. She had three sons and only one lived locally. Dylan had been notified of his mother's condition and was sitting with his mother when I entered the room. He was a young man in his early twenties and seemed upset and agitated. I was immediately concerned whether or not he was receiving enough support to cope with his mother's dying. I did not have to worry for long because, shortly after my arrival, a veritable parade of professionals, from Vivian's psychiatrist, case worker and the director of nursing for the nursing home to our own hospice nurse came in and out of the room. In the brief hour or so of my visit, many necessary details were sorted out, the most important being that Dylan was able to absorb the reality of his mother's dying. Vivian's caseworker offered to phone his brothers who lived out of state, while Dylan made arrangements to take at least a few days off from his job.

Over the course of the next two days, Dylan hardly left his mother's side. His brothers were doing their best to get there, but it was unclear what arrangements they were making, as both had limited financial resources. I came in to relieve Dylan on both those days so that he could go home, shower and put on fresh clothes. Vivian was now in a deep coma, and the nurses were surprised that she had hung on for this long. Dylan was convinced she was waiting for her other two boys to arrive. But apparently, this was not the case. Vivian died just before dawn on the third day, with her youngest son Dylan faithfully keeping the vigil. Vivian made it home in good time for Christmas.

Keys for Creating Compassionate Care for the Dying

Identify and respect coping mechanisms. Smoking can be a coping mechanism for the patient. Just because patients have been diagnosed with lung cancer or respiratory failure, does not mean they will be inclined to quit smoking. Patients may give themselves internal permission to carry on with life-long habits by rationalizing that they are going to die soon anyway. Sometimes, as in Vivian's case, this permission was shrouded in ambivalence. We need to respect individual choices even when they clash with our own values. Accepting diverging values not only reinforces patients' dignity and selfhood, but it also gives them a sense of control when so much about their situation is beyond their control.

Keys for Hospice Volunteers

Get the right fit. Finding a good match between a patient and a volunteer is critical in providing quality hospice care. In order for the volunteer coordinator to determine the best volunteer for a particular assignment, communicate any restrictions you may have with regard to placement. For instance, you may prefer not to be around smokers, you may have pet allergies or you may not be able to travel long distances. On rare occasions, the hospice staff may have to remove a volunteer from an assignment because the home environment is deemed unsafe. I know of only a few cases where this decision was made—one in which a caregiver and patient did not wish to correct a potential fire hazard in their home and a second where loaded firearms were discovered in the house.

13

SAYING NO TO MORPHINE

It was a spectacular Montana summer. We enjoyed one big sky of blue after another, with enough rainfall to maintain a verdant green backdrop to endless fields of alpine flowers. After many summers of drought and wildfires, this July was a welcome reprieve. It was during this time that I received a call from Ellie, about a friend of hers named Ruth. I knew both women from my husband's church community. Ruth had recently celebrated her 90th birthday a few months ago and my children and I visited her with flowers, balloons and a card in tow. I'd been friends with Ruth for a decade and over the years we would visit at various church functions. We also visited in the hospital, where she was admitted periodically with complications from emphysema. Decidedly independent, Ruth lived alone for many years. She was very committed to her faith community and was well loved by many. Ruth had a daughter, Marion, who visited her regularly from Arizona, as well as other relatives scattered around the map.

Ellie was relieved to reach me and gave me a synopsis of what was currently happening. Recently, Ruth's health started declining significantly. She was hospitalized for a week with respiratory difficulty and because Ruth's physician did not feel it was prudent for her to return alone to her condominium, she was then transferred to a nursing home. Marion came to be with her mother and, after consulting with the physician, both Ruth and Marion determined that Ruth should move into an assisted living environment, where she could receive help with personal care and meals, and be more closely monitored. In the past, when she went through similar health crises, Ruth had made it clear to her friends and family that she enjoyed her independence and was not ready to give up her condominium. Even though moving into the assisted living facility was a decision she made with her daughter, it was a decision that she would later regret.

Ruth had been in the assisted living facility for almost three weeks and her health continued to decline. Her breathing was becoming more labored, because her medications were no longer effective in managing the emphysema. One evening her physician paid a visit, confronting Ruth on the finality of her illness. She explained that there was nothing else that could be done to cure her illness and that at this stage, Ruth would be best served by hospice. According to Ellie, who was present during this exchange, the physician was as blunt as she could possibly be. Ruth was dying from emphysema and comfort measures were all that could be offered from now on. The physician called Marion and gave her the same information. At this point everyone was struggling with varying levels of grief and loss.

How did Ruth's independence impact her ability to come to terms with her end-stage illness?

Since Ellie was aware of my hospice experience, she had called to get my input. Ruth was having a hard time processing this latest conversation with her doctor. Though regular updates were shared with her faith community about her well-being, Ruth did not want people to know she was dying. Her physical frailty, together with her inability to handle visits from friends in the community, made it difficult for anyone beyond her immediate circle of companions to see her and say goodbye. I told Ellie I was relieved to know that a referral to hospice had been made and I was confident the hospice nurses would do their best to keep Ruth comfortable. Ellie then suggested that I might want to confer with Julia as well.

Julia is a minister from Ruth's church and one of Ruth's closest companions. As with Ellie, Julia had been closely involved in the sequence of events that brought Ruth to this juncture. Julia was preparing to leave on a trip the following morning and would be gone for a week. I got through to her that evening and she shared more details with me. Although Ruth had asked for her daughter's assistance in determining the most appropriate living arrangement, she was not at peace with her current circumstances. Ruth expressed her need for spiritually minded people to be around her and that it was hard to be dependent upon caregivers that she did not know. In hindsight Julia wondered if it might have been a mistake not to allow Ruth to return to her condominium, if only for a little while. Moving from the hospital to the nursing home and then directly to the assisted living facility did not allow Ruth to experience a sense of closure in her home, a home which served as a vital symbol of her independence and selfhood. The advancing disease, coupled with its debilitating symptoms, triggered a series of events that left Ruth feeling as if life, as she had known it, had been snatched away from her. Ruth was frustrated and needed to reclaim some semblance of control over her situation. Since she had never explored alternative living environments and because her health was deteriorating so rapidly, Ruth was psychologically unprepared for the transitions she now had to face.

> What happened to Ruth when her chronic illness transitioned into a terminal one?

Seeing hospice as yet another decision/transition to be made, Ruth was ambivalent about it. To complicate matters in Ruth's mind, hospice was associated with opioids, like morphine, and it was Ruth's understanding that her church strictly prohibited narcotic use. Ruth had shared her concerns about morphine with Julia, and in turn, Julia passed this information onto me. I asked Julia if she thought it would be helpful if I called Ruth's daughter, who I had met several years ago during one of Ruth's hospitalizations, and fill her in a little bit about hospice and the services it offers. She thought that was a good idea and gave me Marion's phone number. I wished Julia well on her trip and told her I'd contact her if there were any significant changes in her absence.

The final phone call I made that evening was to Marion. She did not remember me, but was grateful for my call and my input about hospice. I relayed Ruth's concerns about morphine; Marion was not aware of her mother's strong convictions. Then she told me about her recent back surgery and how she was given morphine for pain relief, immediately following the surgery. She had no side effects, nor any difficulty weaning herself off it to a less potent analgesic. Marion said she would explain all this to her mother when she saw her. She was planning to return to Montana within the week, as soon as she could arrange her schedule. I offered to visit Ruth the next day and get some more input about her feelings. Marion asked me to let her know how it went. This was Thursday evening.

On Friday morning I spoke with the hospice social worker and she confirmed that they had received a referral for Ruth; she also indicated that a dilemma was brewing between the administration at the assisted living facility and Ruth's physician over the issue of catheterization. The administration maintained that they were not adequately staffed to properly oversee a catheter for Ruth and, in such cases, typically recommended transferring to a skilled nursing facility. However, the physician saw no need for a catheter at this stage, though certainly one might be necessary down the road. Since this was Friday, the social worker did not anticipate Ruth would be admitted onto hospice until Monday or Tuesday of the following week. I knew that Ruth's doctor was leaving on vacation that afternoon and was concerned that the issue be resolved before her departure. Another move, back to the nursing home, would be terribly hard on her and I wanted to do everything possible to avoid it. I was also anxious about Ruth's rapidly deteriorating respiratory condition. Both Ellie and Julia had observed that her breathing treatments and current medications were no longer effective in keeping her comfortable. If her doctor was out of town, and hospice services were not yet in place, would her symptoms be adequately managed in the interim?

When I spoke with Marion about the situation, she said that she had left several messages for one administrator at the assisted living facility with no response. She finally got through to an assistant who was aware of the issue concerning the catheter, but had not heard any discussion about a possible transfer. I encouraged Marion to be firm with the administration in her desire to have her mother remain where she was. She emphasized that she was not easily intimidated and had no problem communicating her expectations to the staff. Marion's confident demeanor reassured me that Ruth could not have asked for a better advocate.

That afternoon I paid a visit to Ruth. She was sitting up in her chair, preparing to eat a light lunch that one of her friends had prepared for her. I told her I wouldn't stay long, but that I wanted to see how she was doing, acknowledging that she had to face a lot of transitions in these recent weeks. "Yes, indeed," Ruth replied, trying to catch her breath. When I asked her if she had any questions about hospice, she immediately brought up her concerns about morphine. I gently, but clearly, reiterated the information her doctor had given her—we could no longer slow the progression of her emphysema, but we could do our best to keep her comfortable. Utilizing carefully monitored doses of morphine would not knock her out, but simply allow her to breathe without so much struggle. There would be no risk of addiction in her case, as her body would use the morphine as an analgesic. And finally, addressing her strong spiritual foundation, I asked if it wouldn't be better for her to focus on prayer rather than on how she was going to find her next breath?

Ruth took in what I said and shared that it was a relief to speak about this with someone who truly understood the spiritual dimension of what was happening to her. Ruth's doctor spoke bluntly about death; I spoke about transitions. I think both terms were necessary for her to integrate. Julia was well trained to help her friend prepare for the spiritual aspects of her dying, but first Ruth had to accept the finality of her prognosis, and in this regard she kept hedging her bets. It's understandable that she was having difficulty coming to terms with her imminent death. Ruth had been living with chronic illness for years. She had explored various alternative therapies, which were successfully integrated into her physician's plan of care. Though winters were typically difficult for Ruth, she had made it through yet another one, but her health was sorely depleted and she never regained her footing. In previous years Ruth always managed to bounce back; part of her was still determined that this time would be no different.

In regard to the morphine issue, she was not ready to make a decision one way or the other, so I said that was fine. I assured Ruth that hospice would respect her wishes and encouraged her to share her perspective with the hospice social worker and nurse during their interview next week. Then I kissed Ruth goodbye and left her to her meal.

It was resolved that Ruth could remain where she was, without the catheter. She was admitted into hospice early the following week. I received a call from Julia soon after she returned from vacation. Several of Ruth's relatives were in town to see her, and during this time it was determined that she would begin receiving morphine. This decision was made with Ruth's consent, after she experienced a severe panic attack while struggling for breath. Even though she consented to the morphine, Ruth still felt troubled about it, and brought it up with Julia, who assured her that the beliefs of their faith community did not prohibit her from taking it, or any other prescribed medication, to relieve the labored breathing. Julia went on to remind her that church members were praying for her and would continue to do so.

A few days later, at Ruth's request, the staff at the assisted living facility called Julia, since they were not able to reach Marion. When Julia arrived, Ruth was distressed and again asked whether she should be taking the morphine. Once Ruth calmed down, they were sitting on the bed, with Julia supporting her to help ease her breathing. Just then two of Ruth's relatives arrived and an upsetting confrontation ensued. These relatives had just been visiting Marion and apparently believed that it was Julia who had been telling Ruth not to take morphine. They sat with Ruth and told her that she needed the morphine to be comfortable, that she should not have to go through these distresses because her family did not want her to suffer. One of the relatives then indicated that Julia go out into the hall with him. He told her that the family wanted Ruth to be comfortable and to take the morphine. He warned her that if she did not stop interfering with the family's wishes, he would invoke "family only" visiting privileges. Julia felt stunned by his anger, as if the wind had been knocked out of her. She assured him that she was not interfering. She had been called in by the staff that evening and, after listening to Ruth's ongoing fear about taking the morphine, she had immediately called Ruth's daughter conveying this information. Julia explained to the relative that she had reassured Ruth that the beliefs of her faith community did not prevent her from taking needed medication. Declining the morphine was solely Ruth's decision and Julia was simply supporting Ruth and her right to choose as best she could. The relative then said that Marion also wanted her mother to have the morphine and he did not want Julia to interfere with the family's wishes. The episode left Julia shaken. She called me and relayed what had just transpired.

> Ruth's family did not want to see her suffer. While trying to alleviate her physical suffering, did they exacerbate her emotional suffering?

The following morning, Julia spoke with Marion who confirmed that she had indeed told this relative that she did not want her mother to suffer. He said he would take care of it, and because Marion was feeling so emotionally drained, she turned the matter over to him. She also explained some of the background behind his

> How can close friends of the dying become disenfranchised by the patient's family?

confrontation with Julia the previous evening. Apparently, his wife had belonged to the same church as Ruth. She died of cancer years ago and was receiving hospice care toward the end. After his wife died, one of her friends, who was another church member, told their young daughter that her mother would not go to heaven because she took morphine. Ruth had known about this story all these years and had believed it. This was apparently the root of her fear and anxiety about taking morphine. Upon hearing these details, as a minister of the church, Julia apologized to Marion for the misrepresentation of the church's beliefs that has led to such a tragic set of circumstances, both past and present. Watching Ruth go down the same path as his wife must have triggered a great deal of unresolved grief and anger for this man, which fueled his outburst with Julia. With this information in hand, where did Julia go from here? She had made a commitment to Ruth to uphold her decision, but had been unaware of the family history that was now erupting. Clearly, the misinformation from this past experience was creating a conflict of wills in the present, and Julia was stationed right in the middle of the crossfire. This group of relatives (except for Marion) left the next day, but Ruth's situation did not get any clearer.

A couple of days later, I received another call from Julia. The staff was now giving Ruth medication, which included morphine; if she asked what it was, they were telling her it was "breathing medication." Ruth suspected some deceit and began telling Julia how upset she was that people were not respecting her wishes. After discussing the situation, Julia asked me to contact hospice to see if they could intervene. After relaying the details to the hospice social worker, she inquired about the church's doctrine concerning morphine and about why Ruth would continue to believe it was spiritually harmful for her. As far as I understood, the church's leadership had never made a distinction between taking narcotics for recreational purposes and taking them under medical supervision for palliative care. Though Julia and I had tried to explain this distinction to Ruth, her beliefs were firmly rooted and she was therefore unable to let go of her fears. At this point, Ruth's clarity was impaired by the disease process and probably by the medications as well, so it is understandable that she would have difficulty reevaluating her beliefs about this issue. The social worker offered to relay the information to Ruth's nurse, who was scheduled to visit later on that day. Though I was hopeful that with hospice's input Ruth's wishes would finally be respected, matters only seemed to get worse.

It turned out that it was Ruth's hospice nurse who had suggested that the morphine be disguised as breathing medication. The hospice nurse, Marion and Julia discussed this outside Ruth's room. The nurse explained her actions by saying that the morphine *was,* in fact, breathing medication and that it was only administered for severe pain or severe breathing distress. For the nurse, it was simply unconscionable to allow Ruth to suffer to the extent that she would if she had not been receiving it. Because I was questioning her actions by way of contacting the social worker, my role in all of this was called into question. Marion and the hospice nurse believed I had misrepresented myself as a hospice volunteer. Although I was intervening as a friend, my affiliation with hospice led to some confusion about my role in Ruth's case. Both Marion and the nurse felt that my level of involvement was out of line. Julia tried to explain that she was the one who had contacted me, on Ruth's behalf, and it was she who had asked me to convey Ruth's concerns to hospice. Based on this conversation, the decision to continue on with the morphine was upheld.

> How do boundaries come into play in this situation?

Ruth was in a deep sleep when I came to see her the last time. Another hospice nurse came by to put in a catheter. Ruth was bed bound now and was no longer eating or drinking. Julia administered the Last Rites to Ruth and I whispered my goodbyes. Tomorrow I would be going on vacation and I knew it was highly improbable that Ruth would still be alive when I returned. I gave Julia a big hug and reminded her to take care of herself.

I received word that Ruth passed away quietly four days later, with her daughter by her side. A few weeks later I was visiting with the hospice manager. He gave me some feedback he had received from Marion concerning me. Marion had attended an IDT meeting while her mother was receiving hospice care. During the meeting Marion made a vague comment about me that caught the hospice manager's attention. When Ruth's portion of the meeting was over, he accompanied Marion out into the hallway to inquire about her comment. Marion did, in fact, want to let off some steam about me. She did not feel comfortable with my involvement. She again mentioned that I had misrepresented myself as a hospice volunteer and felt that I had tried to exert too much control over her mother's care. The hospice manager was very objective in delivering this feedback and I appreciated his sensitivity.

Giving it some thought and mentally reviewing our few conversations, I recognized that the problem between Marion and myself might have stemmed from our phone conversations before she arrived. At that point I was concerned about Ruth being able to receive hospice care where she was, without having to transfer to a skilled nursing facility. In hindsight, I recognize that I might have been too forceful when encouraging Marion to speak up to the administration in support of her mother. Having become more familiar with Marion subsequent to these initial conversations, I can easily see how she may have been put off by my assertiveness. Based on her first impression of me, it is not surprising that she would later draw the conclusion that my intervention was out of line, when the conflict arose about the morphine.

I was grateful for this feedback, though saddened that my actions had contributed to an already stressful situation. Sorting through the details of Ruth's final days has made me aware that sharpened communication skills are not only necessary with patients, but with family members as well. Perhaps if I had been less caught up in my concerns over Ruth's care, I would not have come across to Marion as having such a strong agenda. Again, it is a matter of balance between caring for and advocating for someone, yet not overstepping boundaries.

When it comes right down to it, my wanting Ruth to receive hospice care where she was and not have to be moved again was irrelevant. I tried too hard to influence a decision that was not mine to make.

But what happens when the wishes of the patient and the wishes of the family collide? With respect to giving Ruth morphine under the guise of "breathing medicine," I personally do not agree with this approach and wanted to advocate on her behalf. Ruth had indicated that she might change her mind if the pain became intolerable, yet the decision was taken out of her hands, and with it, any last measure of control over the life she had left. Ruth died with her breathing successfully managed, but was it at the expense of her dignity and selfhood?

Coping with Conflicting Roles and Values

While creating compassionate care for the dying, we will at times encounter complex situations that present numerous dilemmas. This episode, more than any of the others included in the book, demonstrates a complicated, interwoven sequence of events that is neither easily read nor interpreted. When the wishes of a patient and the wishes of the family collide, a complicated tug of war can ensue. In the case of Ruth, whose wish not to take morphine to relieve her pain was opposed by her daughter and nurse, consider the challenges that each of the individuals involved in the situation had to face:

Ruth's challenge: Finding physical relief versus suffering and dealing with increased mental and emotional anguish as a result of her beliefs regarding morphine

Marion's challenge: Wanting to alleviate her mother's breathing distress versus respecting her mother's religious beliefs

Julia's challenge: Upholding her commitment to serve as Ruth's advocate versus knowing that Ruth's beliefs were based upon a tragic event from the past that involved a misconception

Hospice nurse's challenge: Wanting to provide palliative care for her patient versus respecting her patient's right to refuse treatment

Mary Jo's challenge: Trying to use her knowledge and experience to support Ruth's companions and to advocate on Ruth's behalf versus having restricted access to the hospice team as an accustomed resource because she had not been assigned to the case as a volunteer

Many of the situations caregivers and hospice volunteers find themselves in will be equally abstruse. Whether we are professionals, volunteers, patients, families or friends, we are all on a learning curve—because we are all human. Although we may strive to create the ideal situation for our loved ones and those we serve, sometimes we will miss the mark. Don't be discouraged when this is the case. Learn from every experience and do the best you can with the decisions you face in the moment. Some circumstances are beyond our ability to control or to understand.

Keys for Creating Compassionate Care for the Dying

Find the best home away from home. Assisted living facilities are communities for seniors who have difficulty living independently. They provide a moderate level of personal care, such as assistance in bathing, preparation of meals and taking medications. Although they are a good choice for frail, elderly people who can manage with some help from aides, overseeing a patient's medical requirements may present some difficulty. When an individual at an assisted living facility is enrolled into hospice, typically the patient and family want the patient to remain at the assisted living facility. If family or other caregivers are not available to provide the additional care needed as the individual's condition naturally declines, it may become necessary to transfer patients to a skilled nursing facility.

Consider morphine for breathing distress. Although morphine is usually used for pain management, it is also effective in easing breathing distress.

Keys for Hospice Volunteers

Be clear about your role. Volunteers who participate in situations involving hospice services for friends or loved ones may find themselves in an ambiguous role. Most of my involvement in Ruth's case centered around serving as a resource and support person for her primary companions and acting as her advocate when contacting the hospice social worker regarding the morphine. However, because I was not involved as a hospice volunteer, my access to the team was limited. To protect the patient and prevent miscommunication between you and others, be clear about the particular role(s) you are playing and the inherent boundaries involved. Tell those you are working with why you are involved and what you see as your role.

14

FAMILY VIGNETTES

GOODBYE TO A FATHER

My dad had a cousin named Joe who was a few years older than my father. They both spent most of their lives in NYC. They had a close relationship over the years and, until recently, would meet regularly at the sailboat lake in Central Park. Since his retirement, my dad's main hobby has been building model sailboats, which he takes to the lake to sail. When Joe came to visit at the lake, Dad would entertain his cousin with his latest jokes. One day, during the summer of 2001, Joe told my dad that he hadn't been feeling too well lately and had gone to his doctor for tests. Initial tests revealed that Joe had lung cancer, while subsequent tests confirmed brain cancer as well. Still, Joe's outlook was upbeat. He was not going to let this news change his lifestyle. An avid tennis player for many years, he continued to play every day. The next time Joe showed up at the lake, he told Dad that he was feeling great. The chemotherapy and radiation hadn't slowed him down at all. He kept up with his exercise regimen and, aside from the predictable hair loss, Joe remarked that he never felt better. This was in September. By the end of November Joe was starting to weaken from his latest round of chemotherapy. Then quite suddenly his hip began bothering him, making walking difficult and painful. This unexpected episode landed Joe in the hospital, never to return home.

Despite a battery of tests to determine the cause of Joe's unrelenting pain, nothing conclusive showed up. Finally, Joe's oncologist concluded that his aggressive radiation and chemo treatments had ultimately compromised Joe's immune system.

At this point I became involved. When Dad phoned me with the news that Joe was in the hospital, experiencing considerable discomfort, unable to get out of bed and basically not eating, I phoned Joe's son, Tom.

Unlike Dad and Joe, Tom and I were not close growing up. Although as a child, I have vivid memories of Joe and his wife Bea visiting my parents, I have hardly any memories of their only son. Tom was my older sister's age, so they kept in touch regularly over the years. Nevertheless, I wanted to offer my support to Tom and his family, as well as any information that might be of assistance to them at this time. We started communicating by e-mail.

I think initially it was hard for Tom to see such a drastic change in his father. One week, Joe was feeling great and playing tennis; the next week, he was stricken with pain and could barely walk. Although the chemo/radiation treatments initially may have slowed the cancer's spread, the cancer was now suddenly gripping him like a vice. When the illness was first diagnosed that summer, Joe told his son that the oncologist believed an aggressive protocol could not only arrest the cancer but might also bring about a cure. That may have been what Joe heard and wanted to believe, but in reality, Tom was told that the average life expectancy for a patient with lung and brain cancer is six months. And as it turned out, that's exactly what Joe had.

> What are some things that Joe may have been hoping for?

Bea was Joe's constant companion in the hospital, doing her best to raise his spirits and coaxing him to eat. She hoped that if Joe could just get some strength back, he might be able to come home again. Tom visited his father several times a week, working around his college teaching schedule. Through our e-mails I offered Tom some information about the importance of palliative care for Joe. Often family members feel helpless in the face of their loved one's pain and trust the medical staff to keep on top of it. If the terminally ill are so caught up in their physical suffering, it is all but impossible for them to approach the emotional and spiritual work of their dying. So I encouraged Tom to closely monitor Joe's pain and to be assertive with the hospital staff in making sure he was receiving the best possible palliative care. Once his physical pain had been abated to tolerable levels, Tom could then focus his efforts on becoming a reflective listener.

I explained that as Joe began dealing with the reality of his dying, he would most likely want to talk with someone he could trust. Whenever Joe was strong enough, I encouraged Tom to be available to his father, as his heart guided him, and use open-ended questions if opportunities arose. Were there any lingering issues between them that needed clearing up? Did Joe have anything he needed to share about his marriage with Bea? Were there any regrets about his life? Did Tom have anything he needed to share with his father? Questions like these are part of the life review process. When we can undertake this inventory with the support of friends and family, there is much opportunity for reconciliation, healing and forgiveness, within one's self and with others. And so these were the two pieces of advice I offered Tom in caring for his dad: to serve as an active listener for Joe and then to advocate for his father's needs and desires with the hospital staff.

E-mail reports from Tom related the unpredictable, up-and-down roller coaster ride, which is often typical of the dying process. Some days Joe would be alert, communicative, have some appetite and even a bit of humor. Thankfully, Tom was able to share a few of these days with his father resulting in several in-depth and meaningful conversations. However, on other days, Joe seemed despondent and would not eat. Battling both physical and emotional pain, the only comfort for him was sleep. As I mentioned with my visits to Lisa, the day-to-day changes in a patient's condition can be hard on family and friends, especially when one is still clinging to hope, whatever form that hope takes. Hope for more time, or even for a good day. Hope to begin that much-needed conversation. Hope for reconciliation and forgiveness. Hope to be free of pain. Hope to be alert and present in the dying process. The list is endless and so, unfortunately, is the unpredictability of whether any or all of these hopes will be realized.

One issue that surfaced during Joe's illness centered around Joe's food. As Betty's and Rudi's stories showed, feeding the terminally ill and knowing when to quit can be one of the most challenging aspects of caring for our loved ones. In Joe's case, Bea was determined to build up her husband's strength in the hope of gaining more time. Whether it was the result of the cancer and the drugs he was taking, a symptom of his depression or a combination of both, Joe's appetite was slight and sporadic. Bea was at the hospital every day, persistently encouraging Joe to eat. The more she pushed, however, the more he resisted. Falling back on her role as nurturer and insisting that Joe eat may have been the only way Bea felt she could take care of her husband at that point. Her efforts, though well meaning, resulted in a power struggle that was undeniably painful for both of them.

I was surprised to learn that Joe's physician had ordered a drug to stimulate Joe's appetite. I wondered if Joe had actually wanted this drug or whether it was prescribed in response to Bea's anxiety over her husband's diminishing need for food. Hopefully, Joe's physician had discussed the issue with both of them. It is far better to educate and offer options that are realistic and appropriate to the disease process than to overmedicate or_simply ignore the problem because "the patient is dying anyway."

Once so upbeat and positive, as Joe navigated his course through end-stage cancer, his mood changed dramatically. Reports from my father indicated that Joe was deeply depressed, but Tom had another take on it. Tom saw his father withdrawing from the world of the living, exhibiting less and less interest in the people and environment around him. Joe knew his days on the tennis courts were over. What else did life hold for him? Perhaps when he realized that his body was giving out, he saw no reason to fight on. Could Joe be happy buying extra time, if it meant relying on a walker or wheelchair, knowing that he'd ultimately end up bed bound again? Tom concluded that his father knew his limitations and what constituted a reasonable quality of life. Although Tom was certain that Joe was "very irritated about all the bullshit of being in a hospital and irritated at having to endure physical diminishment, he did not feel entitled to 'more life"—he wanted to go." The trade-off of a tennis court for a walker just didn't cut it and, whereas my dad may have read this as giving up, Tom definitely saw it as a natural letting go.

> Can you identify the stages of dying that Joe passed through? Was Joe experiencing reactive or anticipatory depression? Or possibly both?

Right after Christmas, Joe was transferred to a nursing home. The idea was that perhaps getting him out of the hospital and providing him a change of scene might help lift his spirits and give him some incentive to start walking again. I don't think he made it a week in the nursing home before his wife had him transferred back to the hospital. Joe was not receiving adequate care at the nursing home, according to Bea. Once back in the hospital, she was finally able to realize that Joe was not going to get better, not even for a little while, not even a little bit. Bea realized that her husband was dying. She understood that the best way she could help him now was to discontinue all tests and treatments and begin the hard work of letting him go. Having crossed this threshold, Bea consented to his transfer into a hospice facility.

The pressing question in Tom's e-mail at this point was "How long?" Although I couldn't answer this, I was able to send him some information about common physical and emotional-spiritual-mental signs of impending death.

> What are some things that Bea may have been hoping for?

I was planning a trip to NYC in early January and discussed with Tom the idea of joining him for a visit with Joe. We decided to schedule it for Sunday, the day before Joe's birthday. Early that morning, at my parents' apartment where I was staying, I received a call from Tom. Joe had died around midnight. Tom and I spoke for a long time that morning. I listened as he explained some of the details of his father's last days and their time together. We spoke about his acceptance of death and his lack of fear, even though he was not a man of faith, in the traditional sense of the word. Tom explained that Joe's creed was living a good and decent life and treating others as he would want to be treated—the simple and timeless Golden Rule.

Tom expressed his appreciation for my support. Although I never had any contact with Joe directly while he was dying, I am grateful that Tom and his family could benefit from my experience. It is sadly ironic that although the hospice facility where Joe was ultimately placed also served as a teaching institute for palliative medicine, when awake his pain was never satisfactorily managed, according to Tom. It saddens me that this experience of watching his father suffer will most likely influence Tom's own attitudes toward death and dying. If we are ever going to transform how our culture perceives and deals with death, we need to better address the pain and suffering of the terminally ill. In doing so perhaps we can instill a greater sense of hope and trust within our society. Then when our own time comes, we can face our dying more honestly and openly, rather than continually reinforcing the denial and avoidance-related responses that are so rampant whenever the topic of death and dying is broached.

Later, when I asked Tom to comment on my account of his father's death, he had this to say, via e-mail, about his experience of watching Joe suffer:

> Certainly, I worked to see how to alleviate his suffering. However, as a believer in the Law of Nam-Myoho-Renge-Kyo (a sect of Buddhism), I was not overwhelmed watching my

> father suffer, because I knew that he had karma to expiate and I constantly thought that he lived in superb health for 83 years and was undergoing (what amounted to) seven weeks of abject misery. I would never generalize about the process of dying in a negative way, because everyone's karma is different. My attitudes toward death and dying are that the focus on enlightenment is especially crucial in one's last hours and days, whether or not the patient is in great pain. I am heartened by stories in my religion of practitioners' last moments. My attitude did change in one way, perhaps: if I get some very serious disease, I will not have chemotherapy and probably won't have radiation. These things are more poisonous than they are helpful. Herbs and vitamins, etc., would be preferable, even if nothing would really help some situations.

It is noteworthy to consider the relationship between the depth of one's faith and the quality of one's dying experience. It is tempting to draw the conclusion that someone with strong religious or spiritual beliefs would have an easier time with death. But consider the person who believes that certain emotions are sinful. How is their dying going to be impacted by feelings they will not acknowledge? Also important is the faith and beliefs internalized by the loved ones. With regard to Tom's comments about witnessing his father's suffering, it is clear that he had a solid belief system in place that allowed him not only to make sense of Joe's suffering, but also to do what he could to alleviate it. Joe, on the other hand, did not have any religious affiliation or system of spiritual beliefs to fall back on. Nevertheless, Tom observed that he did not have any fear of death. These were Joe's comments eight days before his death: "If I'm not going to get better," (and according to Tom, Joe didn't think he would) "then I'd rather it [death] be sooner than later. It would be

If a patient is repressing certain emotions, how can this exacerbate the pain and suffering of dying?

sad for your mother and you, but it would be good for me." Tom reported that he said this calmly, without bitterness. Other comments also indicated a lack of fear of death, and Tom was grateful for his father's outlook: "If Joe intended to influence me, that's the attitude I want to have when I'm facing departure."

On occasion, I've sat with patients whose spiritual beliefs were in direct contrast with their friends or relatives, as in Lisa's situation. These are issues around which the hospice team must walk very gingerly. Obviously, the hospice chaplain or spiritual care coordinator can and should be called in these instances, when desired by the patient and/or family. But in Joe and Tom's case, they negotiated each other's beliefs with the utmost care and respect, much to their credit.

Emotional Side Effects of a Hospital Death

Specific issues may surface for those who spend their final days in a hospital. In her book *Talking About Death Won't Kill You*, Virginia Morris has this to say about the emotional side of dying in a hospital setting:

> Another difficult aspect of dying today is the emotional toll. Psychological pain is difficult to measure or study, but interviews with doctors, nurses, families, and patients suggest that for a majority of people, dying is not only prolonged and needlessly painful, it is also lonely and frightening. In the hospital, patients are demeaned by the power and complexity of the institution and the technology therein, they are dehumanized by a web of tubes, wires and intravenous lines, and they are invaded regularly by hospital staff who take blood samples and check monitors and medications at all hours of the day and night. Patients often become depressed and anxious, symptoms that are often left untreated. The trouble is, physical pain exacerbates psychological pain, and vice versa,

> so the patient is drawn into a downward spiral of deepening depression, distress, and pain (p. 31).

I believe two qualifiers to Ms. Morris' comments are in order. First, overall awareness and sensitivity to these issues is heightening among hospital staff, and many hospitals are now offering palliative/comfort care consultations. In addition, patients enrolled in hospice who spend their final days in a hospital setting are usually closely monitored for these symptoms by the hospice staff. Medicare guidelines stipulate that hospice needs to oversee the plan of care for their patients when they are admitted to hospitals and all other in-patient facilities.

Although physicians and hospitals are gradually addressing these issues, more work needs to be done. Yet we shouldn't think that we are helpless in this regard. We each have the ability and responsibility for decisions concerning end-of-life care. We can start with educating ourselves about all the options rather than assuming that "authority figures" will have all the answers. Take time to think about the hard dilemmas you and your family may face *before* a crisis hits. As a good starting point, go back to the keys in this book and study the resources and books listed in the appendices.

Keys for Creating Compassionate Care for the Dying

Closely monitor pain relief. Helping patients manage pain in the final stages of life is essential. Studies have consistently shown that terminally ill patients in hospitals receive inadequate medications for pain relief. Research demonstrates that the majority of people today die in pain. One such study was the Study to Understand Prognoses and Preferences for Outcomes and Risks of Treatment (SUPPORT). It included more than 9,000 patients with life-threatening diseases at five U.S. hospitals, making it the largest study of dying ever undertaken. The study found that 50 percent of those dying were conscious at the time, and half of that group were in moderate to severe pain most of the time. Virginia Morris writes in her book *Talking About Death Won't Kill You* that many of the surveyed patients suffered from the terrifying symptom of shortness of breath and that "most struggled with other agonies as well, including confusion, nausea, skin sores, constipation, infections, dry mouth, and itchy skin." Morris also says, "When Dr. Joanne Lynn, the lead investigator of this study, looked within her own hospital in Washington, D.C., she discovered that more than a quarter of patients also died with their arms lashed down at their sides to keep them from pulling the tubes that so irritated them" (p. 30). Make sure that pain levels and symptoms are accessed regularly, ideally whenever vital signs are taken. There are several different pain assessment scales typically used in hospices and palliative care facilities.

Respect a patient's rights and desires. Some patients may purposely choose pain and suffering as something they must experience. They may associate meaning and even redemptive value with their suffering. Under these circumstances, pushing for pain control can actually negate the patient's rights and desires. Teaching and offering patients all appropriate options and then respecting their wishes is the ultimate goal in providing comprehensive, compassionate care.

Practice reflective listening. By engaging patients in supportive dialogue and listening to them closely, we may be able to illicit information that could help them gain closure and peace of mind. For example, we may be able to pick up cues about pain levels, symptoms, side effects from treatments, spiritual concerns or any other basic quality-of-life issues. Don't force these conversations. Instead, always allow the patient to take the initiative. Here are a few examples of how a family member or friend can use open-ended questions and reflective listening to help a patient:

Joe: "I can't wait for this to be all over."
Tom: "Tell me more about that."

Joe: "I don't know what's going to happen to your mother."
Tom: "Are you concerned about how mom will get along without you?"

Joe: "My brother and I haven't spoken in years."
Tom: "When was the last time you were in touch?"

Joe: "I wish I could just go home."
Tom: "It's hard staying here at the hospital."

Take a closer look at depression. Depression can provide the impetus for the dying to come to terms with a life that is ebbing away, helping them find resolution and closure. Joan Furman and David McNabb delineate two forms of depression in their book *The Dying Time*—"reactive depression" (reacting with appropriate sadness to losses that have already occurred, such as the loss of control over changes in our body) and "anticipatory depression of impending loss" (for example, the loss of a dream of retiring or of something a patient had planned for the future). "This anticipatory depression is an introspective sadness that helps you prepare to leave," they write. "In this stage you may find yourself not wanting to talk, but preferring to touch or to visit quietly. It is time to probe and to respect your need for introspection" (pp. 105-106).

Recognize the five emotional stages of dying. Not only is it difficult to accurately interpret the emotional world of the dying, but if family members have conflicting viewpoints about what is going on, the situation can be even harder to address. Often the best solution is to acknowledge the discrepancy in views and encourage tolerance of both points of view. In addition, learn to recognize the five emotional stages of dying, outlined by Elisabeth Kubler-Ross, M.D., the esteemed pioneer in the field of death and dying: denial, anger, bargaining, depression and acceptance. Unfortunately, many people misinterpret this model as a linear progression. However, Kubler-Ross explained that how and in what order these stages are experienced is unique to each individual. She also said that the stages can be revisited more than once during the course of a terminal illness.

Keys for Self-Care

When the going gets rough, get help. It is not unusual for life-long patterns of behavior (such as Bea and Joe's power struggle over food) to crescendo among family members during an end-stage illness. Stress levels are high and time is running short. Behaviors and issues that may have characterized a relationship are not automatically going to go away. Calling on the help of an auxiliary team of professionals trained in death-and-dying issues can greatly support a family. Even when no formalized programs are available, people will often step forward to offer help, like the male nurse who spoke with James and me the evening James was admitted into the hospital. His sincere and compassionate support was invaluable. Be open to seeking the services of a grief counselor or social worker. This kind of intervention could make all the difference.

FOLLOW YOUR INTUITION

My grandmother Sandra had been living in a nursing home in NYC for the last six years. My father and brother persuaded her to leave her apartment when her thinking became delusional, a symptom of her advancing dementia, and she was no longer able to take care of herself. The last time I had seen my grandmother was at a family brunch to celebrate my recent wedding. Grandma seemed frail and much quieter than I remembered. During my childhood and into my adult years, Grandma was always the main attraction at any family gathering. Decked out in designer dresses, with her white hair superbly coiffed, she made a formidable impression. Sandra was well traveled and politically opinionated, so she could keep any conversation going at an ample clip.

I never knew quite what to make of Sandra, our family matriarch. She seemed far too glamorous and self-absorbed for my notion of what grandmothers should be like. In fact as a child I remember asking my father (her only son), if she was a movie star. Although I did spend time with her while growing up, I never really warmed up to her. Maybe it was because she always seemed to favor my sister, or because I sensed my mother's dislike of her, or maybe it was because she reigned over my father in ways that I perceived as very destructive. Probably for all of these reasons, and maybe some others, I kept my distance.

However, in the winter of 2000 I found myself thinking of Sandra often, experiencing strong inner promptings to visit her at the nursing home. So I made plans to visit NYC with my daughter that spring. My idea was to have a family reunion at the nursing home, but as plans sometimes go, that one was a bust. My mother, who never changed her opinion of Sandra, did not want any part of it. My sister

> In respecting my intuition, did I impact Sandra's dying experience?

declined to come as well, as she was not on speaking terms with my brother. That left my brother, my father, my daughter and myself, which was just fine.

On a Saturday morning my brother picked us up and drove to the nursing home. I had been to nursing homes many times during my years as a volunteer, but this was the first time I would actually be visiting a member of my family. I wondered how it would be different from all the other visits. My father recognized a couple of the attendants and asked how his mother was doing. A number of months ago, Sandra's speech had become unintelligible, a result of the dementia. She spent most of her days, I was told, sitting in her wheelchair at the nurses' station, cuddling a favorite stuffed animal. She would recognize my father, but just barely. Once her speech was gone, this left little room for interactions between mother and son. My father's visits tapered off. Dad would phone the nursing home regularly to see how Sandra was doing. The most recent reports indicated that she was starting to decline—sleeping more and eating less. Today, in response to Dad's inquiry, the attendant said pretty much the same. Sandra's condition was deteriorating.

> Could Sandra have called me to her bedside to say goodbye? Was this encounter between us her gesture of atonement?

As we entered my grandmother's room, I saw her curled up, asleep on her bed. It had been five years since I had last seen her and over six years since she first moved into this nursing home. These people were her family now, the ones who knew her best and who cared for her. I sat gently at the edge of her bed and quickly scanned the room. I saw a few personal items—a picture of her grandchildren, a plant my brother most likely brought her on his last visit. Today he came bearing a beautiful pink hydrangea. I reminded my brother that Sandra loved flowers and would especially love these big, luscious blooms. I like to associate flowers with people's personalities and this showy hydrangea was a perfect fit for my grandmother.

After taking in her immediate environment, I gently started stroking her hair. In a quiet voice close to her ear, I called her name and tried to rouse her. Dad then came over next to her, and started to shake her awake, almost shouting the news of our arrival. I was concerned that he would startle her, and that she would awaken feeling disoriented and agitated with all these strange people gathered around her bed. She finally stirred and looked at me. I told her who I was and her eyes started to sparkle. She smiled and tried to speak to me. I smiled back and told her how glad I was to see her. It was clear that she recognized me and was very happy that I had come. Then I gestured to my daughter, who was four years old, to come over to the bed. I told Grandma that this was her great granddaughter, Fiona. Again her eyes shone with sheer delight as she gingerly reached her hand toward Fiona's face. Within moments, Sandra's eyes were starting to drift closed; soon she curled up again into her peaceful sleep. This greeting, kindled through our eyes, lasted no more than a minute or two, yet it was probably the most loving connection I ever felt with her. It was a profound reconciling of our lives together. In every sense of the word, for me, it was a miracle. Though I could have continued to sit quietly in her room, the rest of my group was anxious to leave, so I kissed my grandmother's forehead and said goodbye.

> As with Lucia, how did Sandra communicate when words were no longer accessible for her?

Back home in Montana, five days later, Dad called to say that Sandra had just died. She was 97 years old. Soon after my visit, the nursing home had transferred Sandra to the hospital when they saw signs of hemorrhaging and internal bleeding. After getting off the phone with Dad, I immediately phoned the hospital to speak with the nurse who tended to Sandra. When I introduced myself as Sandra's granddaughter, she gently offered her condolences, which I appreciated. I asked her about Sandra's dying. She got her chart and explained that the bleeding was probably the result of prior surgery many years ago for colon cancer. Sandra's living will had stated that no extraordinary measures be taken to prolong her life, so there was never any consideration of transfusions or surgery to stem the bleeding.

I then asked the nurse how my grandmother seemed before her death. She said that initially Sandra was agitated and disoriented, not realizing that she was in the hospital. But after that, she seemed to settle down and slept quietly. Sandra probably went into shock, from loss of blood. The nurse said that when she went into her room that morning to check in on her, she was dead. Notes on the chart from the previous night indicated that Sandra was quiet and comfortable. From the nurse's accounts, it was a peaceful, painless death. As deaths go, Grandma got a good one. Not knowing whether any family members were intending to come to the hospital to say goodbye, the nurse kept Sandra's body in the room for a couple of hours and went in herself to say a prayer. I was deeply moved and grateful for this nurse's love and sensitivity. Not only had she taken the time to review Sandra's chart with me, but she had also obviously given her tender care as well, both prior to and following death.

No more than a couple of hours after learning of Grandma's death, I walked over to the neighborhood grocery. As I was approaching the entrance, a woman walked past me who had a striking resemblance to Sandra. I was stunned. When I returned home, just a few minutes later, there was a beautiful deep pink azalea plant on my doorstep. The attached note said that my friend had received this as a gift. Not being good with plants, she wanted me to have it. I knew it really came from my grandmother—a sign to say that all is well.

How did this nurse help me to grieve the loss of my grandmother?

Keys for Creating Compassionate Care for the Dying

Follow your intuition. Intuition is a valuable gift that can help you respond to the needs of the dying. Following your intuition can benefit both you and the patient. Use your intuition generously and act on your inner promptings.

Keys for Self-Care

Look for signs. Acknowledging signs from our loved ones after they have died not only helps with our grieving but can also reaffirm our belief in the continuity of life. Not everyone believes in an afterlife, so be prudent who you share your experiences with so that the value of these precious pearls are not tarnished in your heart.

EPILOGUE

✦

THE CIRCLE OF LIFE

It's been a year since that crisp autumn afternoon, when I first began writing this book. This morning as I sit at the computer, icicles shimmer in the frozen air. It is mid-winter now and my life has been blessed with many changes, including the imminent birth of my second child.

These months of pregnancy have given me insight into the similarities between living with a terminal illness and living with a baby growing inside you. Quality of life issues are a huge concern for the dying. There are so many symptoms, changes and losses to adapt to as the disease invades more and more of the body. Some individuals collapse into depression when faced with what seems like the insurmountable. But other individuals seem to maneuver through these changes with more equanimity and grace…why?

As the months of my pregnancy progressed and my belly expanded, I needed to make some necessary and obvious adaptations. I had to eliminate more and more clothes out of my wardrobe. For some women, clothes aren't a big deal, and although I always shop at consignment and thrift stores, I enjoy a great variety of clothes to pick from on a daily basis. My maternity selection is very limited and not that exciting. For me, it was a loss.

A long-time student of yoga, I had to continually change my practice, replacing my more challenging and satisfying postures with gentler ones. And even though these adaptations were ultimately in my own (and my baby's) best interest, I initially struggled with them. I discovered that I had allowed my self-esteem to become too attached to some of the more advanced postures, so that when I could no longer safely do them, I felt my current yoga practice wasn't as "good." And therefore I didn't feel as good about myself in doing the practice. Another loss.

Last winter my daughter began taking skiing lessons. I was never much of a downhill skier: speed, feeling out of control and falling a lot all frightened me. But what really terrified me were the ski lifts. I have an active fear of heights, so riding up the hill was not a pleasurable experience. Also getting on and off the lifts was not much fun either. But as I watched and experienced my daughter's enthusiasm for skiing, I wanted to be able to share in her passion. I decided this was a good time to confront my fears and put on some skis. We had a blast. Going up on the lift with her, I felt increasingly more at ease and skiing down the mountain was also more manageable. By the end of the season, I could envision this as a sport she and I could enjoy together for many years to come. But pregnancy prohibited my participation this winter and I was bummed. Another loss.

And then, of course, the random and unpredictable symptoms of pregnancy need reconciling. The most persistent symptom I've had was fatigue. It's hard to feel excited about life when you're constantly running on half a tank of gas. And then, there was the hemorrhoid! I wondered how in the world a woman could give birth vaginally if she had a hemorrhoid? My midwife assured me she had helped women in this predicament. What do you do? Someone just has to put their hand on the hemorrhoid and apply counter-pressure during labor. Talk about dependency and feeling humbled in the face of one's limitations! And then there's morning sickness, nausea and various food intolerances and aversions that are often present. Hormonal changes that play ping-pong with your emotions can be exasperating (and not just for your partner either). The quality of life, even during a good pregnancy, can be very different than what it was before your test strip came up positive.

Of course, many people would argue that comparing living with a terminal illness to living with a pregnancy is simply ridiculous. But the point I am trying to illustrate is that how we approach anything in life—whether it's preparing to die or preparing to give birth—is largely determined by our attitude and focus. We can cling to aspects of our life that were once familiar and safe while denying or fighting off the changes that are systematically overtaking us. We can choose to focus on all the cumulative losses and indignities that greet us at the door of every waking day or we can choose to shift our focus, allowing us to make the necessary adaptations that will ultimately better serve us on the journey.

Life is inundated with many "little deaths"—losses that cannot be recouped. During these transitions we have the opportunity to learn so much about ourselves and the coping mechanisms we typically employ to deal with changes. It certainly seems reasonable to conclude that how we handle these cumulative losses will directly impact how we enter into and experience our dying process. It is my hope that as topics related to death and dying filter more and more into our culture and our own individual awareness, it will be easier for us to integrate into our living, the many wonderful lessons that the dying continue to teach us. In this way, death will no longer hang down like a sword over our heads, as we anxiously try to keep ourselves shielded from it for as long as possible.

A profound gift that I've received through my hospice work is a greater love and appreciation of my family and relationships in general. I've seen people die with a lot of unfinished business and with things left unsaid to the people they love. Issues of forgiveness, towards oneself and others, are also common burdens for the dying. Nurturing healthy relationships and refining my communication skills are now ongoing priorities in my life.

From the dying I am also learning about authenticity and integrity. To hold eye contact with someone close to death is like dipping into the well of our shared humanity—pain, suffering, fear, anger, love, denial, despair, isolation, acceptance, forgiveness, compassion—the list is endless. Letting go of life and all that we love can be a terrifying task. But if we can approach it in stages, doing the "work" and making the necessary mental, physical, emotional and spiritual adjustments along the way, then I do feel that it's not only possible, but altogether probable, to experience a "good death" in whatever terms we would define that for ourselves.

For someone entering the autumn of his life, the question arises: what is death actually like? What if we turned this question around and asked: what is *life* actually like? Certainly we could expect a broad range of responses, based on the individual's attitude and experiences. My hunch is that the same holds true for how we die. What we bring of ourselves to the process will largely impact how the events of our dying will unfold. It has been well documented that it's not so much death that frightens most people, but the ordeal of dying itself. Fears include lack of control, being dependent and a burden on others, facing multiple indignities of a decaying body, uncontrollable pain and suffering, loss of quality of life and loss of self. The ever-evolving science of palliative care has successfully addressed many of the physical symptoms of dying. It is now the exception, rather than the rule, that we will experience unbearable physical pain when we die. The psychological, emotional and/or spiritual aspects of our suffering may be more enigmatic to identify and ameliorate, but again the holistic approach of the hospice team is ideally suited for such tasks. This is why one often hears about the phenomenal potential for healing, intrinsic within our dying. Stephen Levine, renowned for his work with individuals in the field of thanatology (death and dying), supports this premise in the following excerpt from his book *A Year To Live: How To Live This Year As If It Were Your Last* (included in appendix):

> If there is a single definition of healing it is to enter with mercy and awareness those pains, mental and physical, from which we have withdrawn in judgment and dismay. Nothing prepares us so completely for death as entering into those aspects of our lives that remain unlived. We need not die defeated by death, feeling a failure, disappointed, constipated

> with remorse. It is possible to die at peace, mostly without pain, still learning, filled with gratitude (p. 48).

We can also break the dying question in half: what is the dying process going to be like for me; and immediately following my death, what will I experience then? Spiritual traditions, whether Christian, Jewish, Native American or Buddhist, each have specific prayers, rituals and teachings to guide individuals through this passage. Christine Longaker's book, *Facing Death and Finding Hope: A Guide to the Emotional and Spiritual Care of the Dying* (included in the appendix) outlines the Jewish perspective on death. Note the emphasis on the life review:

> The hope offered to a dying person is not that of a heavenly existence after death, but rather in the righteous life he or she has lived on earth. Hope comes from being connected to a living spiritual tradition and its rituals, having used one's life meaningfully, contributing to the community, and helping to care for family and friends…A dying person is encouraged to accept the reality of her death squarely and conclude her life well…While dying, she examines her life, acknowledging and atoning for any harm she has done, and extending forgiveness to anyone who has harmed her (pp. 117-118).

People with no religious orientation can also navigate their dying process quite well, as described in the following quote from Levine's book. He poses that it's not necessarily our spiritual beliefs that will fortify us at the end, but how we've lived our lives, each moment, until then:

> Although I have seen people who opened like exotic flowers on their deathbed seemingly without much preparation, this is not something you can count on. If you examine most of

> these spontaneous openings you will find that many of these people lived their lives with some degree of awareness and at least a modicum of common courtesy. I have seen even those who have long since abjured God die in grace. In fact, there is nothing more beautiful than an atheist with an open heart. Atheists don't use their dying to bargain for a better seat at the table; indeed, they may not even believe supper is being served. They are not storing up "merit." They just smile because their heart is ripe. They are kind for no particular reason; they just love (pp. 46-47).

Addressing the second part of our question, we can draw from the many beautiful accounts of individuals who have had near-death experiences. These episodes happen to people regardless of any particular religious orientation. Though their backgrounds may be vastly different, their near-death experiences have much in common. They speak of moving swiftly through a tunnel toward a bright light and feeling completely enveloped by a spiritual presence (Jesus, Mother Mary, Buddha or another familiar presence) emanating unconditional love; sometimes they are greeted by loved ones already deceased, as with the stories in *Final Gifts*; and always there is a relief from all suffering and pain. When they return from this journey, in most instances their lives are profoundly changed. For many, the two guiding principles that provide the framework of their lives from that point on are these: how well can I love and how successfully can I serve?

From my perspective, the most important consideration is, how do I support someone who is dying as they reflect upon these critical questions? In the chapter dealing with Doug, these issues were agonizing and although there were many attempts by the hospice team to help him find his way through the labyrinth of suffering he endured, Doug never came to terms with the mystery or with the unknown. He could never trust in or surrender to the process. I feel the best we can offer someone dying is our own sense of comfort with death and its essential place in the circle of life. If we are asked specific questions about our understanding and beliefs surrounding dying and death, then we can offer our own perspective. If not, it is important to allow the person their own journey, being as accepting and nonjudgmental of their experience as possible. In either case, it is *their* experience; therefore we must always remain in the background as witnesses, being cautious not to impose our fears or predilections on our patients. Whatever transpires, whether it is a "good death" or not, there is always opportunity for us to learn and grow as well as the potential to bring that much more to the next person we serve.

In his book, *After the Ecstasy, the Laundry: How the Heart Grows Wise on the Spiritual Path*, (listed in the Appendix), Jack Kornfield writes about his father's death in the ICU of a university medical school.

> Later in the evening most visitors had gone and I told my father I needed to sleep. "Don't go!" he pleaded. I sat with him for another hour as he repeatedly drifted into sleep and startled fearfully awake. "I can't sleep. Please, please don't go." I was happy to comply; I've learned to sit. Eleven, twelve, one, two a.m., I sat with him over a number of nights. There wasn't much to say. I held his hand. He was frightened. He didn't want to know about meditation. He didn't even want to talk. What mattered was that I sat there, not being afraid, not rejecting his fear and his pain, and simply holding his hand. He died after several more days. I was grateful to have been able to sit with him during this extraordinary time.
>
> Perhaps this is the best we can do: To help when we can; to witness each other with kindness; to offer our presence; to show the trust we have in life. Spiritual life is not about knowing much, but about loving much (pp.219-220).

I no longer draw boundaries around my spiritual beliefs, affiliations, practices, or rituals, calling this one or that one my "group" or "religion." The benefits of serving as a hospice volunteer have bled into all aspects of my living. The same holds true for my spirituality. When I was first considering becoming a hospice volunteer, I felt a deep sense of urgency to utilize my spiritual knowledge in comforting the dying. Maybe there were certain aspects of my particular faith that would help alleviate their pain and suffering. Now I've come to realize that it's not so much what I believe or don't believe that conveys compassion and comfort toward my patients, but who I am and how I love. And with each hand I hold and each heart I embrace, I know there is no end to the love we share on this remarkable journey from one side to the other.

"Do not despise death, but be well content with it, since this too is one of those things which nature wills…As thou waitest for the time when the child shall fall out of thy wife's womb, so be ready for the time when thy soul shall fall out of this envelope."

The Meditations of the Emperor Marcus Aurelius Antoninus

ACKNOWLEDGMENTS

I am thankful for my elders—the authors whose work I have studied in conjunction with my training in death and dying. Their wisdom and experience have enriched my life. Thanks to Steve Janes for his mentoring, friendship and time in discussing the educational material for the chapter summaries. His dedication to hospice, insightful analysis of the text and gift for detail has blessed me and this book tremendously. Thanks to Les Morgan for critiquing the first edition. His recommendations provided the impetus that led to this new edition. Thanks to Carol Kriegel, Nigel Yorwerth and Patricia Spadaro for their encouragement and confidence in my work. Their collective years of experience in marketing, book distribution and writing have been invaluable to me in preparing this manuscript for publication. Thanks to Marie Lynn for her skillful editing. She remains my primary role model of selfless service. Thanks to Cindy Wilks-Gee for her technical assistance. It saved me considerable time and frustration knowing that she could make the computer do what I could not. Thanks to my husband, Roger, for supporting this project through its many stages. He never once doubted its completion or its value. Thanks to my children, Fiona and Oliver, for giving me time to write. It's hard sometimes sharing your mom with a computer. And thanks to my community of friends and family for their wonderful enthusiasm and love.

Appendix A

RELEVANT TERMS

Respite Care Facility: A facility designed to care for patients, providing short-term relief for family and caregivers.

Hospice House: A facility designed to provide round-the-clock care for terminally ill patients in the event they can no longer receive adequate care in their own home.

Curative Care: Treatment focused on seeking a cure for a terminal illness

Palliative/Comfort Care: Treatment focused on pain management and symptom control; maintaining the individual's comfort and quality of life through a wide array of resources.

Hospice Care Eligibility: a physician's referral, based on a six-month or less life expectancy and the cessation of further curative measures.

IDT: Interdisciplinary Team. The hospice manager, nurses, physician, social worker, home health aide, psychologist, chaplain, pharmacist and volunteers meet weekly to review the current status and plan of care for hospice patients.

DNR: Do Not Resuscitate; an order written into the patient's medical chart indicating that if the individual's breathing or heartbeat stops, no attempt should be made to revive her, either by emergency personnel or hospital staff. Hospice patients will typically have a DNR sticker in a prominent place by their front door.

Palliative Sedation: the monitored use of medications intended to induce varying degrees of unconsciousness, but not death, for relief of refractory and unendurable symptoms in imminently dying patients.

Advance Directives:

1.) Living Will: outlines a person's preferences for medical treatment at the end of life, typically stating that if the person is near death and has no reasonable hope of recovery, he does not want to be kept alive by "heroic" or "extraordinary" means.

2.) Power of Attorney for Health Care: authorizes some other person, usually a family member, to make medical decisions should the patient be unable to make such decisions for himself.

Common Radiation Side Effects: It is helpful to be aware of the common side effects of radiation and chemotherapy treatments. These side effects include, but are not limited to, nausea, loss of appetite, metallic taste in mouth, hair loss, skin changes, fatigue, constipation, diarrhea and inflammation of mucous membranes in the mouth as well as other areas included in a radiation field, such as pharynx, esophagus, trachea, bowel, bladder and rectum.

Physical and emotional-spiritual-mental signs and symptoms of impending death, excerpted from *Preparing for the Death of a Loved One*, by the Metropolitan Hospice of Greater New York:

Fluid and Food Decrease: Be careful of decreases in swallowing ability, and do not force fluids if the person coughs soon after. Small chips of ice, frozen juices or Popsicles may be refreshing in the mouth.

Decreased Socialization: The person may want to be alone with just one person or with very few people. Keep the environment quiet and calm and reassure the person that it is okay to sleep.

Sleeping: The person may spend an increasing amount of time sleeping and become uncommunicative, unresponsive, and difficult to arouse at times. This normal change is due in part to changes in the metabolism of the body.

Restlessness: The person may make restless and repetitive motions, such as pulling at sheets or clothing, or have visions of people or things that do not exist. These symptoms may be the result of a decrease in the oxygen circulation to the brain and a change in the body's metabolism.

Disorientation: The person may seem confused about time, place, and identity of people around them, including close and familiar people. In conscious moments the person may speak or claim to have spoken to people who have already died or to see places not presently accessible or visible to you. This is not a hallucination or a reaction to medication. It signifies a person beginning the normal detachment from this life, preparing for the transition so it will not be frightening.

Incontinence: The person may lose control of urine and/or bowels as the muscles in the area begin to relax.

Urine Decrease: Urine output normally decreases, becomes more concentrated and may become the color of tea. This is due to decreased fluid intake and to a lessening of circulation through the kidneys.

Breathing Pattern Change: The person's usual breathing patterns may change with the onset of a different breathing pace. Breathing may become shallow, irregular, fast or abnormally slow. This is a result of decreased circulation in the internal organs and buildup of body waste products. Elevating the head and/or turning onto the side may increase comfort.

Congestion: Oral secretions may become more profuse and collect in the back of the throat. The person may develop gurgling sounds coming from the chest. These normal changes come from fluid imbalance and an inability to cough up normal secretions. It is helpful to raise the head so that the secretions collect lower down in the throat and won't stimulate the gag reflex. Turn the person's head to the side and allow gravity to drain the congestion. You may also gently wipe the mouth with a moist cloth.

Color Changes: Due to changes in circulation the person's arms and legs may become cold, hot or discolored. This may be especially noticeable in the extremities where the color may change to a darker, bluish hue. This is a normal indication that the circulation is conserving to the core to support the most vital organs. Sweating may occur and there may be an odor resulting from the many physiological changes taking place in the body. The heart beat and pulses may become slower, weaker and irregular.

At the Time of Death: Breathing ceases, heartbeat ceases, the person cannot be aroused, the eyelids may be partially open with the eyes in a fixed stare, the mouth may fall open as the jaw relaxes; there is sometimes a release of bowel and bladder contents as the body relaxes.

APPENDIX B

SELECTED READINGS

Byock, Ira. *The Four Things That Matter Most.* New York: Free Press, 2004

Callanan, Maggie and Patrica Kelley. *Final Gifts.* New York: Poseidon, 1992.

Collett, Merrill. *At Home with Dying, A Zen Hospice Approach.* Boston: Shambala, 1999.

De Hennezel, Marie. *Intimate Death.* New York: Vintage Books, 1998.

Furman, Joan and David McNabb. *The Dying Time.* New York: Bell Tower, 1997

Groopman, Jerome. *The Anatomy of Hope.* New York: Random House, 2004

Heckler, Richard A. *Crossings.* New York: Harcourt Brace & Company, 1998

Hallenbeck, James L. *Palliative Care Perspectives.* New York: Oxford Press, 2003.

Kessler, David. *The Needs of the Dying.* New York: Quill, 1997.

Kornfield, Jack. *After the Ecstasy, the Laundry*. New York: Bantam Books, 2000.

Kubler-Ross, Elisabeth. *To Live Until We Say Good-Bye*. New York: Simon & Schuster, 1978.

_________. *The Wheel of Life*. New York: Scribner, 1997

Levine, Stephen. *A Year To Live*. New York: Bell Tower, 1997

Longaker, Christine. *Facing Death and Finding Hope*. New York: Doubleday, 1997.

Morris, Virginia. *Talking About Death Won't Kill You*. New York: Workman, 2001

Nuland, Sherwin B. *How We Die*. New York: Knopf, 1993.

Quill, Timothy E. *A Midwife Through The Dying Process*. Baltimore: Johns Hopkins University Press, 1996.

Wilber, Ken. *Grace And Grit*. Boston: Shambala, 1991.

Woods, Dillon. *Where Souls Meet*. California: Windmere, 2000.

APPENDIX C

RESOURCES

National Hospice Helpline: 1-800-658-8898

Heart-to-Heart: Caring for the Dying. Three, hour-long audio documentaries, produced and directed by Claire Schoen.
www.hearttoheartradio.com

Primer of Palliative Care, Porter Storey, M.D., 1994. Available from:
The American Academy of Hospice and Palliative Medicine
P.O. Box 14288
Gainesville, Florida 32604-2288
(352) 377-8900.

Hospice Hands, a wisely chosen set of links, updated weekly under the auspices of Hospice of North Central Florida
http://hospice-cares.com
email: healing@hospice-cares.com

Growth House, Inc. improves the quality of compassionate care for people who are dying, through public education about hospice and

home care, palliative care, pain management, death with dignity, bereavement and related issues.
http://www.growthhouse.org

The National Hospice and Palliative Care Organization
http://www.nhpco.org

National Hospice Foundation
http://www.hospiceinfo.org

Hospice Foundation of America
http://www.hospicefoundation.org

The Hospice and Palliative Nurses Association
http://www.hpna.org

Compassion In Action: *The Twilight Brigade* is committed to raising society's consciousness about the needs of the dying through community and professional education, advocacy, and service to the terminally ill and their loved ones so that no one need die alone.
http://www.twilightbrigade.org

Crossings is a resource center for after-death care alternatives.
http://www.crossings.net

Palliative Care Perspectives, by James Hallenbeck, M.D. can be viewed, in its entirety, at Growth House, Inc.
http://www.growthhouse.org/stanford

ABOUT THE AUTHOR

For more than ten years, Mary Jo Bennett has been a dedicated, skillful and sensitive hospice volunteer attending the needs of the dying. Through her years of experience at the bedside of the dying, she has mastered the art of assisting those who are making their final passage through life. She is passionate about helping all who will ultimately lose someone they love come to appreciate and respond to the needs of the dying so they can face death with peace and dignity. By lifting up our culture's awareness of these issues, Ms. Bennett hopes to dispel the myths and fears that shroud the beauty and mystery of death and what lies beyond. She graduated cum laude from Syracuse University in New York and now lives with her husband and two children in Bozeman, Montana.

You may contact her at: thebennetts@montana.com

978-0-595-31662-5
0-595-31662-X